Grandparents
MINNESOTA STYLE

by Mike Link and Kate Crowley

Adventure Publications, Inc.
Cambridge, Minnesota

Dedication:

To Aren, Matthew and Ryan who have taught us
the magic of grandparenting.

You're responsible for your own safety and well-being.
Make good choices out there.

Photo credits:

Cover photos: Gregg Felsen: carousel (back cover left inset), farmer's market (back cover middle inset) **Laura Ingalls Wilder Pageant, Walnut Grove, Minnesota** (back cover middle-right inset) **All other cover photos courtesy of Mike Link and Kate Crowley**

All photos are copyright **Mike Link and Kate Crowley** unless otherwise noted. **Gregg Felsen:** 40, 48, 122, 148 **Historic Chippewa City, Montevideo, Minnesota:** 94 **Jon Kramer:** 90 **Laura Ingalls Wilder Pageant, Walnut Grove, Minnesota:** 92 **Jonathan Norberg:** 138 **Sinclair Lewis Interpretive Center, Sauk Centre, Minnesota:** 96 **Shutterstock:** 13, 15, 17, 19, 20, 82, 110, 128, 140, 156, 160

Edited by Ryan Jacobson

Cover and book design by Jonathan Norberg

10 9 8 7 6 5 4 3 2 1

Contents

Introduction

Grandparents Minnesota Style is designed for today's grandparent who wants to spend more time discovering the world with his or her grandchildren. While we see value in some of Minnesota's larger, more "commercial" options, we prefer locations that offer a little more culture, history and oneness with nature. You won't find places like Valleyfair or the Mall of America in this book, but you will learn why we think you should bring your grandchild to the State Capitol, Pipestone National Monument and even your local library.

This book is about opportunities for adult and child to have fun, laugh and share. Of course, Minnesota is ripe with more possibilities than we can ever cover, but this is a place to get you started. We decided to write this book because of our grandchildren—three boys and a fourth grandkid on the way. They provide us with a lot of fun, but we also have a responsibility to them. We must use our time together to help them learn and grow as individuals.

In successfully doing so, we had to stop and think about the knowledge we've gained through our experiences, how we learned those valuable life lessons and how we could pass our wisdom to our grandchildren. With the changing times, we found that several necessary experiences have become endangered. Some of them include solitude, silence, open space, dark night skies, free time, reading books, family meals and home-cooked food.

Several differences within our society have contributed to our grandchildren's diminished opportunities. Consider the following:

1. In 1900, farmers accounted for forty percent of our census. By 1990, the total fell below two percent. Farms are no longer a part of most children's experiences.

2. Open space was once a playground. Now it is slated for development. Children are left with only fenced yards and indoor locations.

3. The "out in the country" experience is disappearing. Urban sprawl has left us with an hour drive from the inner city to any country areas.

4. Tree climbing is a thing of the past. The trees are all but gone, and lawsuits limit access to just about everything. There is nothing left to take the modern Jacks and Jills up the beanstalk to their dreams.

5. The chance to be bored—which is an opportunity to be creative—isn't in the schedule. Children are signed up for every organized activity and training available, eliminating family time and free time.

6. Sports used to be played for fun. Now we must choose a sport, send our kids to summer camps and act like winning is all that matters.

7. Canning, pickling and baking—all of those wonderful activities that filled the root-cellars and pantries of the past—have vanished.

Think about our earlier years, about all of the things that were so important to our lives and developments. These and many more are gone (or nearly so), and we can only reminisce about their absences: soda fountains, radio dramas, family TV, typewriters, telephone party lines, the ragman driving his horse cart, ice cream trucks and record players.

Today's world has seen some bad and dangerous trends. Pollution has become an industry. Fast food (and obesity) is the norm. Meth and other deadly drugs flood our cities, our neighborhoods and our schools. And that's just the tip of the iceberg.

There are no simple solutions, yet the need for change is quite apparent. Fortunately, our grandchildren have us. The role of the grandparent is very different than it was when we were young kids, and we must adapt too. Here are a few reasons why:

1. Grandparents are living longer than ever before and can guide their grandchildren longer.

2. Parents work long days, filled with busy hours, just to pay for day care.

3. Grandparents can provide children with quiet times, new experiences, fewer electronics and more play.

4. Grandparents can help introduce children to healthier food; we have the time to prepare it and present it.

5. Children need to hear perspectives from someone other than peers and parents. They need our guidance and insight.

It comes down to a need to establish the extended family again, the new nuclear family of the twenty-first century. As grandparents, we must take it upon ourselves to lead the charge.

That's not to say we should take on the role of mother and father. Instead our place is to supplement a child's parents, to help them wherever our help is wanted and needed. Let's use the time we have with our grandchildren to instill them with important values, to teach them about the world around them and to help shape them into better people.

A Word from Mike Link

In an age when "Soccer Mom" and "Soccer Dad" are used as normal terms to describe parenting, our roles and relationships can be confusing. Parents are scheduling rather than parenting, channeling rather than nurturing, coaching rather than modeling. This may not be the parents' choice, but in the driven world we have created, the demands to make a living are great.

Do not despair; there is a solution that is ancient in its lineage. As the *Washington Post's* Abigail Trafford writes, the next two decades will become the transition from baby boomers to grand baby boomers. Good parenting means extending the safety net of support, love, learning and connection through the extended roles of grandparents, aunts, uncles and cousins.

As a child, I spent all of my "non-school" time living with my grandparents in a small town in Wisconsin. My father worked evenings and weekends, trying to get us out of the poverty that surrounded us. It was not a desertion of responsibility on his part but rather a sharing of it. Ultimately, I grew up an "only child" with six parents (my mom and dad, my father's parents, my Uncle Clarence and Aunt Agatha) and with my cousins Elaine and Lois, who became my "sisters."

I think of my childhood, and it is filled with memories of picking blackberries with Grandma and playing catch with Grandpa. I was never a visitor; I felt that their home was my home. This is also what we want for our grandchildren. Our home, our land, our love is theirs, and the wonderful thing is they are ready to give their love in return!

Today's grandparents live longer, have the potential for better health and have more opportunities than ever before to share stories, read books, look at old photo albums, talk about the good old days and enjoy their grandchildren.

Talking, reading and reminiscing are all great, but the stories are wonderful for us because we lived them; the photographs have meaning because we experienced them. If you want to build memories rather than dwell on them, get out there, get going, take your grandchildren and experience the world again through their smiles, their curiosity, their wonder and their energy.

Many times you can include the parents in the activities you share with your grandchild. A multi-generational event can be truly wonderful, but choose a leader beforehand. Is the parent in charge of the activity or is it the grandparent? If there's ever any doubt, step aside. A multi-generational squabble does nothing positive for the child and may be more damaging than good.

The intergenerational escape is a unique adventure. This is the time when we truly share. No one is ever more honest in their emotions than when they are smiling or laughing. No one is less guarded and more accepting of new knowledge than when they are engaged in new and positive experiences.

Grandparents are reflecting pools that have gathered the wisdom of their age and the knowledge specific to their own families. Children need the chance to delve into the pool for consolation and contemplation. It is not the role of the grandparent to solve the grandchild's problems but rather to provide the means by which the child can solve his own questions of value, right and wrong. The grandparent is in the neutral role and needs to hold this position. We are advocates for the parents and for the children.

In a 1996 book, *Contemporary Grandparenting*, Arthur Kornhaber shows the evolution of the individual from his own childhood to grandparenting. The list is worth considering as we work to find the special activities that grandparents should share with their grandchildren:

- from receiving as a child to giving as an elder,

- from being nurtured as a child to nurturing the young,

- from learning to teaching,

- from listening to stories to telling them,

- from being directed to directing,

- from simply reacting to one's environment to becoming able to influence the world and

- from identifying with others to becoming an object of identification for the young.

We are the elders; we are a starting point for more generations—how exciting and how challenging. Don't dwell on it. Just be yourself. Be honest, be fun, and be open. Grandchildren are gifts from the future. The love they have for us, if we are willing to involve ourselves in their lives, is beyond description. Our greatest gift to them is our love and attention, and they are the greatest gift we could ever receive. Through them we can see the decades ahead. They connect us to their world, and we in turn owe them a connection to ours.

A Word from Kate Crowley

If you're lucky, you grew up knowing your grandparents. If you're even luckier those grandparents lived nearby and enriched your life by their interest and enthusiastic involvement. Unfortunately, the Industrial Revolution, while it has brought us lives of relative ease and abundance, has also brought about the gradual decline and demise of the close-knit, extended family.

Much of the knowledge that our elders, the grandparents, carried was tied to life on the land. We can recall the easy, simple times spent with these adults who indulged us and shared their memories of a time that today seems as remote and as removed as the Middle Ages. Yet, since we carry the memories and experiences with us, we have the opportunity to share them with a new generation, being born into a century with untold opportunities and far too many dangers.

As we age, we reflect on our childhoods. Even though the mists of time tend to spray a cloud of gold over those days, we know that there were experiences that gave us great pleasure and cemented the bonds with the elders who shared themselves with us.

When I was born, I had two living grandmothers. One lived in California, and I have very fuzzy memories of her. She only visited us a handful of times, and I don't recall her as particularly warm or even interested in interacting with my siblings or me.

My other grandmother lived just a block away from us, and I had more than twenty years of close acquaintance with her. I even lived with her for four years during and after high school. She didn't have the time or personality to get down on the floor and play with us, but her house was always open to us and we wore a path through our neighbor's back yards to get there. She had a few old toys and books for us to play with and a big, old piano that we made noise on, but mostly we simply came over to visit. If we were lucky, she'd make us root beer floats.

This is what I believe about our most firmly held memories of time with our grandparents: They are tied to our senses, all of which were much keener for us as children. Smell, sight, sound, touch and taste—these are the things that will stay with a child as they grow to adulthood, recalling times shared with grandparents.

One of the most mouth-watering, sensual memories I have with my grandmother is from a summer day, when we went out into the country to pick tomatoes. It was a hot day and even though we got there early, the sun was beating down on us as we moved through the pungent rows of tomato plants. What I remember most about the day is that she packed cheese sandwiches, and I have never eaten anything more delicious than a rich, sweet tomato right off the vine, still holding the sun's heat, juice running down my chin, followed by a bite of soft cheese on white bread. The smells and tastes flowed together, and I can see us there now, joined forever by the simple act of harvesting food.

I have waited a very long time to become a grandmother and not just because our daughters chose to wait until their thirties to have children. I can't explain why, but even when my two children were preteens, I was contemplating grandparenthood. I packed away all of their Fisher Price toys in the original boxes to share with the next generation, and I saved as many of their books as possible. I so greatly enjoyed raising those two children that I knew I wanted to have similar experiences again—but without the many worries and day-to-day concerns that accompany parenthood. I understood even then that, as a grandparent, I would be able to have fun, play, act silly and share what I've learned in life but still have the luxury of going home at the end of the day to a quiet, clean house.

Now we have three grandsons—all of whom arrived in the span of one year—and we are looking forward to years of adventures together. This is why we have written *Grandparents Minnesota Style*: to help other grandparents find those unique and unforgettable places that will combine fun and facts, history and humor, excitement and enduring memories for you and for the special grandchildren in your life.

How to Use This Book

The suggestions in this book are just that: suggestions. Some experiences—such as a canoe trip in the Boundary Waters or a visit to Hawk Ridge—are unmatchable anywhere else in the state. Others can be replicated. If you are not near the museum, park or site that we highlight, find a similar place near you. Read our suggestions, and be sure to pay special attention to each "Bonding and bridging." This is how we believe you can tie your visit to an important life lesson. Take advantage of our advice or come up with your own, but use each opportunity to its fullest!

We do not advocate that you become the "wallet" or the "chauffeur." What we want you to consider is an active participation in friendship and sharing that is enriched by love. We want you to receive the respect of an elder, to exhibit the wisdom of your age and experience, and to enjoy the wonderful love that can flow between generations.

One of the themes of this book is that things change. This is true for everything, including our state's attractions. They sometimes close, renovate or move. When in doubt, *CALL BEFORE YOU LEAVE*.

Canal Park

There's no single place that says, "Duluth," like Canal Park. The lift bridge, the restaurants, the harbor view and the canal encompass the essence of what makes Duluth so unique in the Midwest. This is the place where the great sea voyages of international vessels come to an end, where people line the walkways to wave their greetings at incoming sailors. Canal Park is also the starting point for ships laden with iron ore. It is a place to celebrate sport and industry, inland and coastal.

With a lighthouse on each side, the canal is a picturesque place to begin exploring Lake Superior. Take your grandchild to the Lake Superior Maritime Visitor Center, which keeps track of incoming vessels and lifts the bridge when needed. The center also provides wonderful displays of Lake Superior's history, so you can combine the past with the present and learn about Great Lakes navigation, including stories of sunken ships.

Next, spend some time outdoors. This is one of the most interesting places in the state, filled with history and chances to share a wealth of information. Skip rocks on the lake, walk along the boardwalk, and hike part of the 4.2-mile lakewalk. You don't get many chances like this one—to hang out under the sun in such a beautiful setting.

The lift bridge is likely to be your grandchild's favorite. It was built in 1905 and has adorned postcards and brochures ever since. It connects Duluth's commercial-business section with the long, narrow sand spit known as Minnesota Point. At the end of the point you'll find a small-plane airport, a boat launch, a picnic area, natural dunes, a forest and a swimming beach.

Duluth's canal originally came about as shipping on Lake Superior began to increase. Businessmen on the Duluth side of the harbor were dismayed to see that Superior, Wisconsin's, port was receiving more activity. They decided to dredge a canal through the narrowest part of Minnesota Point. The town of Superior filed a court injunction to halt the dredging and got their ruling. But while the papers were being delivered, the Duluth citizens worked around the clock and had the canal completed by the time the papers arrived. The rest is history!

Bonding and bridging:

Lake Superior is as close as we can get to a coastal experience. From Canal Park, the view to the east is an open horizon. The water curves over the edge of the round earth twelve to twenty miles away, depending upon where you are standing. On warm days, upside-down mirages appear before the vessels and sometimes seem to ride atop the ships.

Imagine the lives led by the sailors on these boats. How and why did they choose their careers? Ask your grandchild what he thinks. Share with him the rewards and dangers of life as a sailor. Then ask what he wants to be when he grows up and what he will do to accomplish that goal. College? Studying? Special training? This is a great way to get your grandchild thinking about how his actions today may affect his success in the future.

A word to the wise:

Standing along the canal when the horns blare and the bridge rises is a wonderfully exciting moment. The incoming ship seems so large that you almost feel as if you can touch it.

Age of grandchild: All

Best season: Summer

Contact: Lake Superior Maritime Visitor Center
(Army Corps of Engineers), 600 Lake Avenue South, Duluth, MN 55802 (218) 720-5260, Extension 1 • info@lsmma.com • www.lsmma.com

Also check out:

Lake Harriet, Minneapolis; (612) 230-6475; www.minneapolisparks.org

Upper Saint Anthony Falls Lock and Dam, Minneapolis; (612) 333-5336 (Army Corps of Engineers); www.nps.gov/archive/miss/maps/model/upperstanthony.html

Grandparents somehow sprinkle a sense of stardust over grandchildren. Alex Haley

Lake Superior Railroad Museum

Do you remember when we were young, when trains were among the most interesting things in the world—the anticipation and excitement of hearing that horn blast in the distance? A train rolling through our neighborhood was a childhood event. We all gathered and waved, hoping that the man in the caboose would wave back. The Lake Superior Railroad Museum has captured some of that magic, allowing us to share it with our grandchildren.

The museum is located on the lower (track) level of the old Duluth Depot, an architectural marvel that serves as home to the children's museum, as well as a repository for one of the great railroad collections. It is significant that the museum is so close to the docks and lift bridge because this is where railroads and water shipping came together mid-continent.

Walking into the high-roofed museum is an amazing experience for you and your grandchild. It does not seem possible to get so many railroad cars in one place, but here they are! A Soo Line caboose from 1886 is the oldest in the collection of red cabooses (and an orange one). Each is distinct and part of the romantic image of the railroad: the black engine roaring in from the distance, the bright red caboose inviting travel and adventure as the train chugs into the horizon.

But as colorful as the cabooses are, it is the collection of engines and small trolleys that will really impress your grandkid. The bulk and the massiveness of the engines can't help but affect any onlooker. In some instances, you and your grandchild can even climb into the cab and feel what it must have been like for an engineer to put his hands on the throttle of such a beast.

What did they do about snow? You'll find locomotive snowplows too. There are many more implements that tell us stories, such as the massive timber loader that cleared some of the forests around Crater Lake in Oregon or the steelworks ladle car that moved molten steel.

There are passenger cars, mail cars and cars of all types, open for your family to step into and discover. Signs help you interpret the past, and models reduce the scale so you can see the big picture of railroading. The models also help the children visualize railroading and are important to their experiences. When it comes to trains, this museum truly has it all.

Bonding and bridging:

It's hard for children to realize how important the railroad was in opening the West and in the commerce of Minnesota. Towns survived if the railroad came through and collapsed if it didn't. This presents an opportunity for you to discuss actions and consequences. There are consequences for most things a grandchild does. Some consequences are good—such as getting an A after studying for a test. Some consequences are bad—like getting an F if she blows off her homework.

Discuss examples of good and bad consequences your grandchild has experienced recently. Ask her what she would've done differently in those situations and how the consequences may have changed. When you do, you'll help her learn to consider consequences before she makes important decisions.

A word to the wise:

Walk the avenue of Depot Square, where the Duluth community of 1910 is recreated. Window shop in the old Duluth Tent and Awning Company, J.L. Tronsdal Meat and Fish, and many more Main Street businesses. This is a wonderful look back at the turn of the century.

Age of grandchild: All

Best season: Summer (when you can walk outside and visit the harbor)

Contact: Lake Superior Railroad Museum, 506 West Michigan Street, Duluth, MN 55802 • (218) 733-7519 • www.lsrm.org

Also check out:

End-O-Line Railroad Park & Museum, Currie; (507) 763-3708; www.endoline.com

Minnesota Streetcar Museum, Minneapolis; (952) 922-1096; www.trolleyride.org

Minnesota Transportation Museum: Jackson Street Roundhouse, St. Paul; (651) 228-0263, Extension 3105; www.mtmuseum.org

Few things are more delightful than grandchildren fighting over your lap. Doug Larson

Great Lakes Aquarium

We live in the land of lakes—close to fifteen thousand of them—as well as ponds, swamps, bogs, marshes and the greatest of the Great Lakes. But what do we know about our lakes? We know we can fish, swim, boat, take pictures and build cabins. Look at the water's surface, and what do you see? Reflections of the sky, the shoreline and yourself. But for as much time as we spend on our lakes, we know very little about what is in them.

The Great Lakes Aquarium is attempting to fill some of that void. It has struggled for funds throughout its startup, so ticket prices are higher than we

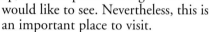

would like to see. Nevertheless, this is an important place to visit.

There is a section of the aquarium devoted to the story of the Great Lakes, and the aquarium is filled with wonderful information that you will not find anywhere else. It is currently Minnesota's only large-scale aquarium, and it has some essential information for understanding the Great Lakes.

The shapes and relative elevations of these lakes are well represented, thanks to the Great Lakes Water Table. It's a real playfest for your grandchild, as he moves floating toy boats through a model of the lakes. Add a few of your own observations to his fun, while learning some new facts yourself.

The main floor features changing aquatic displays that often depart from the freshwater realm, with such exhibits as the Abyss: a combination of aquaria, film and displays. There is also a river otter display and two large, two-story tanks of freshwater fish.

But that's not all. Your grandchild can also touch real stingrays and sturgeons, watch the sea creatures being fed, meet Bogey the Bald Eagle (who has a wing injury preventing him from returning into the wild) and much more.

We love Minnesota for a lot of reasons. The Great Lakes Aquarium is the place to celebrate one of them.

Bonding and bridging:

The Great Lakes Aquarium lifts the curtain on one of childhood's mysteries, revealing a hidden world that lies beneath the water's surface. Suddenly, we're snapped into an awareness that there are things around us which we never before noticed.

The possibilities that come with this realization are almost endless. You can use your time to discuss how our actions affect the environment—how we must be stewards of the land to save these fish habitats from pollution. Share how factories located hundreds of miles away may discharge harmful chemicals that travel to our region in air currents. These chemicals then fall into our lakes as acid rain, killing plankton that small fish feed on, thereby killing the small fish, which in turn depletes the food supply for larger fish.

The overall message here is a big one: Just because we can't see something doesn't mean it won't have a huge impact on our lives or on the environment around us.

A word to the wise:

Everyone loves the action when the big fish are fed. The fish become more active, we can see them use their fins and tails, and they interact more with one another. Feeding times are posted, and each is hosted by a narrator.

Age of grandchild: All

Best season: Summer (because you can combine the visit with so many harbor experiences)

Contact: Great Lakes Aquarium, 353 Harbor Drive, Duluth, MN 55802 (218) 740-3474 • www.glaquarium.org

Also check out:

Minnesota Zoo, Apple Valley; (800) 366-7811; www.mnzoo.org

Underwater Adventures Aquarium (Mall of America), Bloomington; (952) 853-0603; www.sharky.tv

The simplest toy, one which even the youngest child can operate, is called a grandparent. SAM LEVENSON

Harbor Fleet

Duluth is almost in the middle of the North American continent, and it is an ocean port! It is on the largest freshwater lake in the world and has saltwater vessels in its harbor. If that is not unique and worthy of a visit with your grandchild, what is?

At the Duluth harbor, visitors have an opportunity that is usually restricted to ocean communities. The port not only welcomes the ships coming for ore, grain and cement, it also makes three of the most interesting vessels available for you to tour. The Great Lakes Floating Maritime Museum is one of the most unusual museums you will ever see. It consists of real boats—an ore boat, a Coast Guard cutter and a tugboat—still floating in the water.

After watching all of those big freighters come into the canal and pass under the lift bridge, don't you wonder what it must be like inside one? The *William A. Irvin* is there to help you and your grandchild answer this question. After forty years of duty on the Great Lakes, it is now tied to shore. This huge ship is still floating and ready to go to work if needed, but for now it is yours to explore. Show your grandchild where the ore was kept, lead her through the crew quarters, take a peek at the 2,000-horsepower engine, and impress her with the gargantuan size of the boat.

Right behind the *Irvin* is my personal favorite: the tugboat. This World War II vessel has quite a history. It towed ammunition across the English Channel, was sunk near the end of the war, and was raised and recommissioned to work in the St. Lawrence seaway. Finally, it moved into retirement in Duluth.

The third boat is the *Sundew*, a large Coast Guard cutter that took care of buoys and broke up the ice in harbors in Lake Michigan. It was built in 1944 and is afloat with stories. The Coast Guard has been a real safeguard for mariners. Their vessels and the men and women who work them have participated in countless rescues across the oceans and the Great Lakes. Their stories of heroism are an important part of the tour.

Bonding and bridging:

The boats exhibited in the harbor fleet are built in very different ways and for very different jobs. Each has a specific purpose. We move vast loads of iron ore in the big laker, we move barges and boats with the tough but maneuverable tugboat, and the cutter is our lifesaver—a boat of heroism and quiet reliability.

As grandparents, we can help our grandchildren understand that they too have a purpose. They may not be good at everything they try, and that's okay. We must guide them toward finding the skills they possess, so they can discover their talents and realize their purpose in life.

A word to the wise:

Your fleet tour should include a visit to the Lake Superior Maritime Visitor Center in Canal Park. You can combine the maritime museum with a walk along the canal to see the lift bridge and to watch the ships come in. The lift bridge going up and the freighter passing beneath is a magnificent sight that can be found nowhere else in Minnesota.

Age of grandchild: 7 and up

Best season: Summer

Contact: Great Lakes Floating Maritime Museum, 301 Harbor Drive, Duluth, MN 55802 • (218) 727-0022, Extension. 234 groups@decc.org • www.williamairvin.com

Also check out:

American Wings Air Museum, Blaine; (763) 786-4146; www.americanwings.org

Minnesota Transportation Museum, St. Paul; (651) 228-0263; www.mtmuseum.org

Museum of Lake Minnetonka, Excelsior; (952) 474-2115; www.steamboatminnehaha.org

Hawk Ridge
Nature Reserve

Some wonders are worth traveling any distance to behold, and the Hawk Ridge Nature Reserve offers one of those natural wonders. There aren't many places a person can go to see thousands of animals in a short amount of time. Who would believe that it's possible to do so here in Minnesota? Each autumn, kettles of hawks migrate directly over Hawk Ridge, above Duluth.

Hawk Ridge is the site of a natural event that every Minnesotan should see; doing so with a grandchild makes it all the more special. Some hawks tend to soar high in the air and can look like black specks against the clouds, but many others fly close enough that you don't even need binoculars. Plenty of these winged creatures will only travel as far as Iowa or Missouri, but some will reach Central and South America.

Hawk migration begins in mid-August and lasts into mid-December, but the best viewing tends to be in mid-September when the largest concentrations of birds are seen. On a sunny day with a west or northwest wind, you may see tens of thousands of birds. (One September day in 2003 topped all previous records when 102,321 raptors were tallied.)

You and your grandchild are likely to encounter up to seventeen species of hawks. Fourteen are seen regularly, while the other three are found less often. Broad-winged Hawks and Sharp-shinned Hawks rank as the most common.

Bring binoculars and beverages with you, since there are no services atop the ridge. Join the other spectators along the edge of the dirt road near the counting station, and note the displays set up by Friends of Hawk Ridge—a non-profit group that helps maintain and support the ridge's programs and research. A naturalist is also on hand every day, to answer questions and to introduce folks to some of the hawks.

Be sure to pay attention to the smaller fliers in the area too. Since this is a nature reserve there is an abundance of shrubs and trees, which are often filled with songbirds on their way south. You may also be surprised to find dragonflies, mostly blue and green darners, drifting and zigzagging overhead. They too migrate along the ridge.

Bonding and bridging:

Where are those hawks going? That's a question that will likely be on your grandchild's mind. At Hawk Ridge Nature Reserve, it's easy to daydream about far off places. Your grandchild sees the hawks flying overhead, and he can imagine them soaring to entirely different continents.

This is a chance to help foster your grandchild's curiosity about the world. Encourage his eagerness to explore. Ask questions like, "If you could go anywhere, where would it be?" After all, a healthy appetite for visiting new and distant places is key to becoming a well-rounded adult. There's no better way to learn about different places and cultures than by visiting them.

A word to the wise:

Adopt one of the wild raptors that has been caught and banded at the ridge. For a fee (which varies based upon the species), you become the sponsor of the bird. Not only does this help raise money for a worthy cause but your grandchild can also have the privilege of holding the bird and releasing it back into the wild blue. There are few things more thrilling than holding a live predator in your hands, feeling its heartbeat, gazing into its fierce eyes and sharing a sense of freedom as it flies away.

Age of grandchild: 6 and up

Best season: Autumn (September)

Contact: Hawk Ridge Bird Observatory, PO Box 3006,
Duluth, MN 55803 • (218) 428-6209 • mail@hawkridge.org
www.hawkridge.org

Also check out:

Winter eagle concentration on the Mississippi River, Reads Landing to Wabasha; (877) 332-4537 (National Eagle Center); www.nationaleaglecenter.org

Winter trumpeter swans concentration on the Mississippi River, Monticello; (763) 295-2700 (Monticello Area Chamber of Commerce); www.ci.monticello.mn.us

Willard Munger
State Trail

Minnesota is lucky to have the most paved bicycle trails in the U.S.—trails that give you wonderful choices of places to go and terrains to cover. The Willard Munger State Trail spans seventy-four miles of eastern Minnesota's beautiful landscapes, between Hinckley and Duluth. If you and your grandchild enjoy biking, the Munger Trail is well worth checking out.

With sixteen access points (eight with parking lots), the trail has plenty of places to jump on or stop off. For instance, you'll come across the Alex Laveau spur, Moose Lake State Park and Jay Cooke State Park. Plus, there's a big attraction that's waiting for you and your grandchild at trail's end: the Lake Superior Zoo!

The flatness of the trail allows bicyclers young and old to enjoy themselves. The section from Hinckley to Finlayson is very easy to bike, and the land around the trails is a mix of wetlands and forest, while incorporating the famous James Root railroad route that saved so many lives during the Hinckley fire of 1894.

Between Finlayson and Rutledge, you'll find the most rolling part of the trail. As you enter the Rutledge area, you'll notice that the trail is bordered by sand plain prairie, not to mention a beautiful bloom during the summer months. This is also the section of the trail that covers the 1918 fire, commemorated at the old depot in Moose Lake.

Perhaps the most impressive and enjoyable section of the trail is found between Carlton and Duluth. The trail crosses the St. Louis River and a dark rock canyon before passing through Jay Cooke State Park. Deep gullies and dark woods give way to the volcanic rocks that overlook the Duluth harbor. Best of all, it's downhill most of the way.

The Munger Trail was named the fiftieth trail of the month by the Rails to Trails Conservancy in 2000. Its breathtaking scenery and its many beautiful access points make this trail an incomparable place to bicycle with your grandchild. A trip down the Munger Trail is a trip through some of the most amazing spots that Minnesota has to offer.

Bonding and bridging:

Some activities naturally put safety at the forefront of our thoughts. Bicycling is one such activity. We can tell our grandchildren time and again, "Safety first." But they notice what we do far more than they hear what we say.

When you're bicycling with your grandchild, always wear a helmet, and use the stop and turn signals taught in elementary school. If you do these things, your grandchild will follow suit. Hopefully, the safety habits that she learns from you will carry over into her future choices—when you're not there to protect her.

A word to the wise:

Take the spur from the trail to the Jay Cooke Nature Center. You and your grandchild will enjoy hiking over the swinging bridge that goes over a fast and complex waterway. You'll truly appreciate the water rushing between the black rocks, the root-beer-colored water, the white foam of the rapids and the deep green forest. It is a wonderful landscape. Plus, kids get quite a thrill when they realize that the swinging bridge moves under their weight. You'll also find restrooms, a picnic shelter and a small interpretive display here.

Age of grandchild: 10 and up

Best season: Spring and fall

Contact: Minnesota Department of Natural Resources (DNR):
Willard Munger; www.dnr.state.mn.us/state_trails/willard_munger

Also check out:

Great Bicycle Trails; www.great-trails.com

Minnesota DNR (state trails); www.dnr.state.mn.us/state_trails

Minnesota Trails; www.mntrails.com

Parks & Trails Council of Minnesota; (800) 944-0707; www.parksandtrails.org

The charm of a woodland road lies not only in its beauty but in anticipation. Around each bend may be a discovery, an adventure. DALE REX COMAN

Moose Lake
Agate Days

There are so many community celebrations that it would be impossible to list all of them. We live in a state where community picnics, fireworks and parades are relatively common. Agate Days in Moose Lake is among my favorites, so I will focus on that one here. However, you should consider this more of a recommendation to find and participate in the small-town events near you.

The community of Moose Lake is built along the shore of Moosehead Lake. The town includes a campground, a picnic area, a swimming beach and a beautiful city park. Agate Days, held annually during the middle of July, is a celebration of those beautiful rocks and the people who collect them.

Live music and great food are always a part of Agate Days. You'll also find Art in the Park amidst the excitement. Plus, the high school next to the park hosts a two-day gem and mineral show that attracts vendors from all over the country.

Of course, every year, the main event is the agate stampede. Adults line Main Street; for children it's the parking lot by the library. Two dump trucks take their positions at the end of each area; as participants lean against yellow flags, eagerly awaiting the event's start. The dump trucks raise their beds, and the fun begins! The trucks move forward, the gates open, and rocks begin to fall— covering the street with three inches of gravel salted with more than 150 pounds of agates and a hundred dollars in quarters. The cannon goes off and the prospectors are underway. This is the ultimate treasure hunt! Most people win, and those who participate with the right mindset always go home happy.

To set the record straight, agates do not originate in Moose Lake. In fact, you would not find them there if not for the large chunk of continental glacier that moved through the area centuries ago. It left a gravel dump of Lake Superior rocks with an extraordinary amount of agates mixed in. But that doesn't matter to the fine folks of Moose Lake; they just see it as a good excuse to celebrate.

Bonding and bridging:

Most towns that host celebrations such as Agate Days have carried on the tradition for years. It's an annual reminder of what makes that town special. It's a chance for people to take pride in where they live.

Use this opportunity to have some fun, but remember to share with your grandchild the history behind the event. Help him to be proud of his community. After all, it's part of what makes him who he is; it gives him roots. Most importantly, liking the town he comes from is a key aspect to liking himself as he gets older.

A word to the wise:

Moose Lake State Park offers a nice picnic area and swimming beach, but what really makes this place special is the Agate Museum (now part of the park headquarters). Beautifully polished agates, a great timeline of geologic ages and other wonderful geology information will add to your weekend's experiences.

Age of grandchild: 5 and up

Best season: Summer

Contact: Moose Lake Chamber of Commerce, PO Box 110, Moose Lake, MN 55767 • (218) 485-4145
www.mooselake-mn.com/AgateDays

Also check out:

Hill Annex Mine State Park, Calumet; (218) 247-7215; www.dnr.state.mn.us/state_parks/hill_annex_mine

Lilydale Park (fossil hunting), St. Paul; (651) 632-2413; www.stpaul.gov/depts/parks/userguide/lilydale.html

Mineview in the Sky, Virginia; (218) 741-2717; www.ironrange.org/attractions/mining/mineview-in-the-sky

Moose Lake State Park, Moose Lake; (218) 485-5420; www.dnr.state.mn.us/state_parks/moose_lake

Intergenerational Camp

Do you think that summer camp is a thing of your past? Think again. You can return once more, but this time you don't have to go alone; bring along a very special friend—your grandchild. Intergenerational Elderhostel is offered every summer at the Audubon Center of the North Woods, near Sandstone.

For six nights and five days grandparents and their grandchildren participate in a variety of indoor and outdoor activities, offering both entertainment and education for everyone. All that you need is provided: rooms, bedding, meals, transportation and a full schedule of fun and adventure.

With all of the logistics handled by the staff, grandparents are free to focus their attention on their grandchildren. This is an opportunity like no other. You and your grandchild come together for countless bonding opportunities. Discover the wonders of nature. Hike and explore new territories, like a beaver pond or a wetland. March to the tunes of the songbirds, and perhaps even hold one.

This camp isn't all "old person" stuff either. You can step aside and cheer your young one on as she challenges herself on the high ropes obstacle course or the climbing wall. Learn exciting, new skills together such as canoeing on the lake. Play games, laugh and have a great time. Plus, just like at summer camp, kids quickly make new friends, so grandparents have time to socialize with one another too.

Nutritious, delicious meals are served cafeteria-style with entrées to whet both young and old appetites. And don't worry about sleeping in a tent or rickety, old cabin. You and your grandchild will stay in a comfortable dorm room with your own private bathroom.

In no time at all, it's Friday evening. Everyone gathers around the closing campfire, making s'mores, singing songs and writing down addresses and phone numbers before saying farewell to newfound friends.

Summer camp was never this good.

Bonding and bridging:

There's no other experience that'll make you feel quite as young again as a stay at Intergenerational Camp—talk about a flashback! Still, you'll find an even better reason to attend: It presents a special opportunity for you and your grandchild. Instead of being the authority figure, you stand on equal ground. You're not in charge, making all of the rules. You're a camper just like she is. A shared experience such as this is a big step in creating a close relationship. It's a chance for your grandchild to realize that you can be her friend, as well as her grandparent.

A word to the wise:

In December, the Audubon Center offers a Holiday Family Camp. This intergenerational event is open to entire families, each getting its own dorm room which can sleep up to eight people. During the four days of this event, you and your grandchild can participate in some of the same activities offered during the summer—such as high ropes and wall climbing. However, with the right snow conditions, events can include dog sledding, sleigh rides, cross-country skiing and snowshoeing. New Year's Eve is also celebrated in a special, family-oriented way.

Age of grandchild: 9 to 12

Best season: Summer

Contact: Audubon Center of the North Woods,
54165 Audubon Drive, Sandstone, MN 55072 • (888) 404-7743
audubon1@audubon-center.org • www.audubon-center.org

Also check out:

Boundary Waters Canoe Area Wilderness; www.bwcaw.org

Elderhostel, Incorporated; (800) 454-5768; www.elderhostel.org

Wolf Ridge Environmental Learning Center, Finland;
(800) 523-2733; www.wolf-ridge.org

Bringing up a family should be an adventure, not an anxious discipline in which everybody is constantly graded for performance. MILTON R. SAPERSTEIN

27

Mille Lacs
Indian Museum

Not much is taught in our schools about the great people who lived in Minnesota before European settlers arrived, but it's important for children to know as much as they can about Minnesota history. We should introduce our grandchildren to the cultures and traditions of American Indians. The Mille Lacs Indian Museum is a great place to start.

The Minnesota Historical Society owns the Mille Lacs Indian Museum, which is located along Highway 169, north of Onamia. But it is staffed by tribal members of the Mille Lacs Band of Ojibwe. It may be quite a thrill for your grandchild to meet a real Indian, and he will likely be surprised to find that American Indians are just like everyone else. They live in houses, drive cars and go to work.

Inside the museum, take a tour of the magnificent Four Seasons Room. This circular space of walls has been painted in a diorama style to reflect the four seasons of the year. Life-sized, realistic figures pose in front of these images, as if momentarily pausing from their traditional activities. Birds perch in trees, a wolf peers from the woods, and a fire burns in a wigwam.

The other exhibits in the museum are a combination of current and historical displays. Many are interactive, something that will please and entertain your grandchild. Local artists and artisans are often found working in the brightly lit front of the museum. These individuals are happy to explain what they are doing, and sometimes visitors can even try their hand at a craft.

Before leaving, take your grandchild next door to the trading post. You will find a variety of crafts and souvenir items, ranging from trinkets to exquisite, handmade moccasins and baskets. Hand-harvested wild rice is often available too.

An excellent introduction to the Ojibwe people, the Mille Lacs Indian Museum provides us with an opportunity to teach our grandchildren about a proud, diverse culture. This is one chance that we shouldn't pass up.

Bonding and bridging:

Ask your grandchild what American Indians are like, and he's likely to tell you that they live in tepees, wear feathers in their hair and shoot arrows at people. Where does he get these crazy ideas? From television and movies, of course!

A trip to the Mille Lacs Indian Museum is about more than introducing your grandchild to another culture. It's about teaching him the negative aspects of stereotyping. He assumes that American Indians were (and perhaps still are) violent and scary. Of course, this was never the case for the Ojibwe Indians. Talk with him about stereotypes and how they can harm others. Would he like it if people judged him without getting to know him first? This conversation will help to create in him an awareness of other people and their feelings, and he'll become a much better person for it.

A word to the wise:

Mille Lacs Kathio State Park north of Onamia is a wonderful place to see the land of the native cultures that thrived in this area. Its nineteen archaeological sites lead you from the early copper period to the time of the Dakota and the Ojibwe. This was a place of settlement long before the Europeans came. According to Ojibwe oral tradition, a three-day battle between the Dakota and Ojibwe was fought here, resulting in the Ojibwe taking possession of the region. Trails and interpretive materials help you discover these stories, and the state park is a wonderful place to hike and enjoy nature.

Age of grandchild: 7 and up

Best season: Summer

Contact: Mille Lacs Indian Museum, 43411 Oodena Drive,
Onamia, MN 56359 • (320) 532-3632 • www.millelacsojibwe.org

Also check out:

Grand Portage National Monument, Grand Portage; (218) 475-2202; www.nps.gov/grpo

Treaty Site Historic Center, St. Peter; (507) 934-2160; www.nchsmn.org

Our children grow up so fast. Maybe grandchildren are God's way of giving us a second chance at participating in the miracle of life. UNKNOWN

29

Hinckley
Fire Museum

Sometimes we have to confront the hard stories, the real stories—not the artificial, slam-bang action of video games, movies and television—but the more poignant stories of people facing threats to their lives, their families, their homes and their communities. The Hinckley Fire Museum offers us a chance to teach our grandchildren about perhaps the greatest tragedy in Minnesota history.

On September 1, 1894, several fires were already burning near Hinckley. It was one of the driest years on record, and tree debris left smoldering by loggers only added fuel. Two of the larger fires joined and turned into an incredibly intense firestorm, which claimed 418 lives en route to destroying six towns and four hundred square miles of land—all within four hours.

The Hinckley Fire Museum puts you and your grandchild there. Imagine flames that soared so high they could be seen in the Twin Cities! Gaze at the vivid colors of the mural. Watch the movie. View the artifacts. It all contributes to a reality that is hard to imagine but impossible to ignore.

Talk to your grandchild about the heroism of train engineers, hands on the throttle, their cars loaded with people, the heat so intense that the windows burst, the steel rails turning soft, the wooden ties exploding into flames. Imagine standing during the middle of the day, surrounded by darkness, of fire raining all around you, of thunder booming in a dry sky—nails melting, animals seeking shelter, humans not knowing which way to turn. It is a terrifying yet important chapter in Minnesota lore.

As a side note, I should also mention that the museum resides in a restored 1894 St. Paul and Duluth railroad depot, housing artifacts from the railroad era. But the main attraction remains the events of Hinckley's tragic fire.

The museum is a great place for you to share with your grandchild your admiration for the survivors and your sadness for the victims. You may even feel anger about the careless waste of forest that led to this tragedy. Most importantly, this fire exhibit is a reminder of the will to go on, to rebuild and to start over.

Bonding and bridging:

The events surrounding the Hinckley Fire are truly sad. However, as with most tragedies, the fire also brought out the best in some people—demonstrating tremendous courage and a will to live. You should focus your grandchild's attention on these attributes.

Tragedies occur every day, from car accidents close to home to the attacks of 9/11 in New York. It's how we respond during these terrible events that make us who we are. You can only teach your grandchild the joys of living and a compassion for others. That way, if tragedy ever strikes nearby, you can count on her to do the right thing.

A word to the wise:

While in Hinckley, visit the "pit," one of the places where circumstances converged to allow deer, bear, humans and other creatures to survive side by side, with fire and blackening clouds all around them. Next, pay a visit to the Hinckley Cemetery east of town. With the lines of four trenches and the towering monolith, it is a dramatic reminder of the day's events.

Age of grandchild: 9 and up

Best season: Summer

Contact: Hinckley Fire Museum, 106 Old Highway 61,
Hinckley, MN 55037 • (320) 384-7338 • hfire@ecenet.com
www.hinckleymn.com

Also check out:

Depot and Fires of 1918 Museum, Moose Lake; (800) 635-3680; www.mooselake-mn.com/Depot

Lake Superior Railroad Museum, Duluth; (218) 733-7519; www.lsrm.org

North West Company Fur Post

Step back to a time when French-Canadian Voyageurs traveled on foot and in canoes, when beaver was their quarry. You've arrived in central Minnesota between the late 1600s and the mid 1800s, and you're about to enter the North West Company Fur Post.

The post, which is just west of Pine City, is a great place for children. Inside the visitor center, your grandchild can walk through the exhibit halls that feature interactive displays. He's welcome to touch some of the furs that were such an important commodity for Voyageurs and traders, and he can watch videos that describe the amazing people who struggled to survive in the wilderness. It might even be possible to play a favorite, old-time game like cat-and-mouse or ball-and-hoop.

A costumed guide leads you out of the visitor center and along a path to the old stockade post. All the while, he shares with you his knowledge of day-to-day life back then. A birchbark wigwam is the first stop, where there is almost always a smoldering fire burning. Farther up the path, you come to the post

itself. In summer, a vegetable garden is planted just outside, looking much as it would have hundreds of years ago. As for the post itself, long logs create a large building that was the home and store for the Voyageurs and for the North West Company's employees.

Drift from room to room with your guide interpreting the artifacts, the tools on the walls, the bedding on the bunks, the table settings and even the toys in a basket. The really nice thing about this "museum" is that it's hands-on. You can touch the items around you and get a sense of how people lived long ago—a big plus when you have a grandchild along.

After you've toured the exhibits, wander along the 1.5 miles of trails through the woods and along the Snake River. It's the perfect way to end an afternoon of exploring this Minnesota landmark. Seeing how the Voyageurs lived, trekking around the outdoors as they would have done, that's the way to make these memories last.

Bonding and bridging:

Grandchildren are too often told to keep their hands off. Don't touch that. Stay away from there. It can squash their curiosity. But it's nice to know that places such as the North West Company Fur Post are still around. The hands-on approach, allowing your grandchild to wonder, to touch and to feel, is how to keep a young mind alive.

Curiosity is a healthy part of development. It should be fostered and developed. After all, where would we be without curiosity? Still living in caves? Encourage your grandchild to be curious, to ask questions and to seek new answers. Do this well, and he might just invent the next "big thing"—which could make all the difference in the world.

A word to the wise:

Come for the North West Company Fall Gathering, held each September at the post. This event features reenactors, who live the lives of early settlers and explorers. They set up tents and traditional shelters, cook over open fires, and make and sell goods—all the while competing for the title of best all-around Voyageur. Enjoy the traditional music and participate in hands-on activities. It's fun to wander among them and eavesdrop on the conversations. Ask questions, and be sure to stick around for the festive dance on Saturday night.

Age of grandchild: 5 and up

Best season: Early autumn (it's cool and there are no bugs)

Contact: North West Company Fur Post, 12551 Voyageur Lane, Pine City, MN 55063 • (888) 727-8386 • nwcfurpost@mnhs.org www.mnhs.org/places/sites/nwcfp

Also check out:

Grand Portage National Monument, Grand Portage; (218) 475-2202; www.nps.gov/grpo/

Historic Murphy's Landing, Shakopee; (763) 694-7784; www.threeriversparkdistrict.org/outdoor_ed/murphys_landing

Oliver H. Kelley Farm, Elk River; (763) 441-6896; www.mnhs.org/places/sites/ohkf

Gammelgarden

In 1972, local residents of Scandia had a wonderful vision. They began the Gammelgarden project in order to preserve the past for the benefit of the future. As a result, one of the country's best places to celebrate Scandinavian heritage was born.

Gammelgarden is particularly important for families with Scandinavian ancestors, since it preserves the home of the first immigrants who settled in Minnesota. The site also includes an old parsonage, a corn crib and a barn. The project culminated with the *Valkommen Hus*, a two-story structure that provides office space, a wonderful boutique gift store, a classroom and restrooms to serve the growing number of visitors.

Volunteers work as guides and provide both information and a welcome. But the real treat is walking into the buildings, letting yourself drift back in time and helping your grandchild connect to an era without electricity.

There are many festivals, and any one of them is worthwhile for the entire family. Our favorite is *Spelmansstämma*, but several other events should be noted on your calendar too, including the following:

- **Annie's Coffee Parties**, two Saturdays a month. Relive Annie's parties and storytelling from the pastor's residence.

- **Midsommar Dag (Midsummer's Day)**. Enjoy the festival's parade, crafts and storytelling.

- **Story Time**, Wednesdays in July and August. Children of all ages will be entertained with stories and books.

- **Hearth and Home**, September. Tour the area's historical homes.

- **Lutefisk**, November. Taste this example of true Scandinavian heritage.

- **Lucia Fest**, December. Celebrate at a traditional holiday festival for Scandinavians—a fun and colorful family event.

Bonding and bridging:

You probably didn't live in houses this small and crowded, but your grandparents or their parents might have. How do you share with children the ways that our lives have changed? Your old photos are good, but Gammelgarden is a tangible reference for them.

Were these people happy? What did the children do for fun? What did they eat? Was there a grocery store? These are questions that grandchildren need to have answered. Could you or your grandchild live like this? What else would you need to have? Use this time as an excuse to buy one of the children's books that depicts the life of this time. Read it, then talk about it. For older children choose a young adult novel, and read it together over time.

A word to the wise:

In mid to late August, attend *Spelmansstämma*. It is a great way to experience Gammelgarden. There are arts and crafts for children in the morning, an art fair all day, tours of the buildings, smorgasbord at the Elim Lutheran Church, a band concert at noon and an afternoon of fiddlers, dancers and many other performers. This event brings the grounds to life and even makes those of us who are not Scandinavian feel a little Swedish.

Age of grandchild: 5 and up

Best season: Summer and fall

Contact: Gammelgarden, 20880 Olinda Trail, Scandia, MN 55073
(651) 433-5053 • www.scandiamn.com/gammelgarden

Also check out:

American Swedish Institute, Minneapolis; (612) 871-4907; www.americanswedishinst.org

Heritage Hjemkomst Interpretive Center, Moorhead; (218) 299-5511; www.hjemkomst-center.com

If you don't know [your family's] history, then you don't know anything. You are a leaf that doesn't know it is part of a tree. Michael Crichton

Grand Rounds
National Scenic Byway

Would you like to see the best of Minnesota's transportation, recreation, nature, art and history? It sounds like a week's worth of touring, right? Wrong! The Grand Rounds National Scenic Byway has it all in one interconnected series of parks, lakes, streams and greenways. Walk, bike, paddle or drive around Minneapolis while remaining connected to the natural world.

When I drive visitors from the airport who have never been to the Twin Cities, I like to show them the Grand Rounds. More than anywhere else, this route shows Minnesota's relationship with nature and with our historical heritage. It demonstrates how people and nature can blend and how refreshing, energizing and uplifting that mix can be.

The Grand Rounds is so unique and beautiful that it has been designated a national drive. The route's seven diverse districts include Minnehaha Falls and Creek, the Mississippi River, the Chain of Lakes, Theodore Wirth Park, Victory Memorial Parkway, Saint Anthony Parkway and Ridge Parkway.

Your options here are endless. Drive your grandchild around and point out all of the sights. With older grandkids, we recommend that you hike, bike or even canoe—if you're feeling up to it. Better yet, why not do all three?

For more kinds of fun, take your grandchild on a trolley ride and skate the lakes during winter. You can also visit the Longfellow House, the visitor center for the Mississippi National Riverway, the historic buildings of Nicollet Island and the old Mill City Museum. Let's not forget swimming, golfing, bird watching, smelling the spring flowers, tobogganing and skiing, as well as visiting the gardens, veterans' memorials, natural springs and side trails for adventure and exploration.

There are many possibilities, so you can choose the section that fits your mood, is most appropriate for the weather conditions and is the distance that you want to cover. Return time and again for different experiences. You can build upon each and every visit.

Bonding and bridging:

In the U.S., nothing quite matches Minneapolis's balance between city life and the outdoors. We should be proud of this great city and of this great state, which places such an emphasis on nature and the environment.

Compare Minneapolis with other big cities that your grandchild may have visited. What does she think makes Minneapolis unique? Ask her if she enjoys all of the open, green places in Minneapolis. This simple line of questioning will lead your grandchild to value her natural environment. Nothing makes us more aware of nature's importance than seeing it preserved within a gigantic city.

A word to the wise:

Visit the Longfellow House at Minnehaha Park. The home is two-thirds scale and was built in 1906 to match the Cambridge, Mass., house of Henry Wadsworth Longfellow, author of "The Song of Hiawatha." The Longfellow House is ideal for an orientation to the Grand Rounds. Your grandchild will also find photographs, stories, natural history and general information that will add layers to her enjoyment. Plus the visit inside will help you plan a return excursion to the Grand Rounds.

Age of grandchild: All

Best season: Spring, summer and fall

Contact: Minneapolis Park and Recreation Board Headquarters,
2117 West River Road, Minneapolis, MN 55411
(612) 230-6400 • www.minneapolisparks.org/grandrounds

Also check out:

America's Byways; www.byways.org/browse/states/MN

Explore Minnesota Tourism;
www.exploreminnesota.com/scenic_byways.html

Skyline Drive, Duluth; www.superiorbyways.com

*My grandkids believe I'm the oldest thing in the world.
And after two or three hours with them, I believe it, too.* GENE PERRET

Lake Harriet

Think about a summer evening, sailboats drifting on the lake and people in-line skating, canoeing, swimming and biking. A cool breeze blows in, and suddenly music fills the air. No, you're not in a Hollywood musical. You are at Lake Harriet in Minneapolis—Minnesota's version of paradise.

Walking in this natural setting of flora, lake and sky is a gentle way to connect your grandchild to nature and the earth, so lead him on a leisurely stroll. It's an easy 2.75-mile walk along beaches and boulevards.

Pump some well water into your bottles, and pick up a few treats at the nearby concession stand. Have a picnic, get a little exercise, and then it's time for the main event: a concert.

The bandstand at Lake Harriet brings people from near and far to gather in the grass or on the benches, so they can listen to the sounds of music while

basking in the sun. People of all ages are here, and the music is as varied as the park itself: big band, jazz, rock, pop, symphonies, folk and ethnic music. Plus, the bandshell was constructed with large windows behind the band. While you're watching the show, you can see the lake, the boats and the sky.

Don't get so caught up in the scenery and music that you forget the other main attraction of Lake Harriet: the Como-Lake Harriet Trolley. There is a great deal of romantic notion associated with a trolley ride. These transports connect us to a slower-paced world. A ride in Streetcar 1300 is a trip back in time to the late 1940s. Adding to the experience, the inside walls (above the windows) are lined with vintage ads from nearly sixty years ago.

Lake Harriet is an experience that the whole family can enjoy because it has something for everyone. Swimming, walking, music, a ride and even a little history—you can't go wrong here. This is one adventure in which nature, family and song can blend into a memorable Minnesota experience. It's places like Lake Harriet that remind us why we chose to live here.

Bonding and bridging:

We are a land of lakes, and the phrase "going to the lake" has special meaning for almost every Minnesotan. Minneapolis's city lakes, including Lake Harriet, are assets that attract millions of visitors every year. It is the duty of the lake users to be lake supporters.

As a grandparent, you can pass along to your grandchild the idea that he should leave a place better off than it was when he found it. This can be as simple as picking up some litter he spots along a trail. If your grandchild gets into the habit of doing this, he will develop a respect and a care for the lakes and the parks that make our state a wonderful place to visit and to live.

A word to the wise:

In October, the Como-Harriet Streetcar features its Halloween Ghost Trolley. For just a few dollars, rides are offered every 15 minutes on the Friday, Saturday and Sunday before Halloween and on Halloween night. This little trip in the dark adds a whole new dimension to the experience, and you can create a special tradition prior to the holiday.

Age of grandchild: All

Best season: Summer

Contact: Minneapolis Park & Recreation Board, 1300 42nd Street West, Minneapolis, MN 55409 • (612) 230-6475 • www.minneapolisparks.org

Also check out:

Fairmont Chain of Lakes, Fairmont; www.fairmontcvb.com

Little Crow Lakes, Spicer; www.spicermn.com

Mille Lacs Lake, Isle; www.millelacs.com

Minneapolis Chain of Lakes, Minneapolis; www.minneapolisparks.org/grandrounds/dist_cl.htm

Thomas Owens Park Bandstand, Two Harbors; (800) 777-7384; www.twoharborschamber.com/parks.htm

Minneapolis Institute of Arts

The Minneapolis Institute of Arts is awe-inspiring for kids. I can personally attest to that. As a child I lived just six blocks from the institute, and I spent many hours of many days wandering the imposing hallways—among the Asian collections and past the displayed paintings and sculptures. Now, as a grandparent, this is one of my favorite places to bring my grandchildren.

Part of the charm of the institute is the imposing building itself. When you enter, bring your grandchild past the lion gargoyles, up the marble steps and through the massive columns. There are other entrances, but they lack the same introductory feeling. Sometimes it's good for a child to be overwhelmed by a building—to sense that a place must be important to be so dramatic. That little sense of awe sets the tone for the amazing exhibits that you are about to show your grandchild.

Once inside, you'll find days' worth of exhibits—more than one hundred thousand objects from diverse cultures—and amazingly enough, the institute is still free to visit. Your grandchild will encounter art from different cultures such as Asia and Africa, from different genres such as photography, paintings and drawings, and from different periods ranging from ancient to modern.

Add depth to the grandchild's visit by asking her what she sees and what she likes, as well as sharing some of your own ideas. Take it slow. Spend plenty of time, perhaps even sit in the museum and let her soak in the experience.

If you plan ahead, special exhibits and family programming are sometimes available. The institute often features temporary displays that focus on a specific style or period. However, these generally require an entrance fee. The institute also offers a Family Day one Sunday a month, featuring hands-on art activities, music, dance, storytelling, demonstrations and more.

Most children enjoy art in one form or another. The Minneapolis Institute of Arts has such a fascinating collection that everyone can find something to appreciate. A visit there with your grandchild could make a lifelong art lover out of her.

Bonding and bridging:

Art is an expression of creativity for its creator. But for its observer, art is a search for meaning. When you bring your grandchild to the Institute of Arts, you are opening her up to a new world. Here, she begins the search for deeper meaning. No longer are the answers obvious. Now she must work to discover what she likes—what speaks to her—and why.

Patiently guide your grandchild through the Institute's exhibits. Don't rush. Let her set the pace. Wait until she finds a piece that makes a strong impression on her, then ask why she seems so drawn to it. What does she like about it? What does she dislike? What does she believe the artist was thinking or feeling when the work was created? Of course, these are questions for which we may never know the answers, but it sure is fun to wonder.

A word to the wise:

The Institute's Family Center, located on the first floor of the museum, is designed for children and their families. There are toys, interactive computer kiosks, books, a play area, an eating area, a rest area and a private bathroom. Plus, there are exhibitions designed specifically for children.

Age of grandchild: 6 and up

Best season: All

Contact: Minneapolis Institute of Arts, 2400 Third Avenue South, Minneapolis, MN 55404 • (612) 870-3131 • www.artsmia.org

Also check out:

Frederick Weisman Art Museum (University of Minnesota), Minneapolis; (612) 625-9494; www.weisman.umn.edu

Minnesota Museum of American Art, St. Paul; (651) 266-1030; www.mmaa.org

Tweed Museum of Art (University of Minnesota), Duluth; (218) 726-8222; www.d.umn.edu/tma/

Walker Art Center, Minneapolis; (612) 375-7600; www.walkerart.org

Mill City Museum

What do Gold Medal, Robin Hood, Pillsbury and General Mills have in common? They are the flour mills that gave Minneapolis its first nickname: the Mill City. These mills made up the financial base of the city, and they marked the introduction of the breakfast cereals that adorn grandchildren's tables today.

The Mill City Museum is another of Minnesota's amazing historic sites where participation is encouraged. Get your tickets, wander around the old train cars, then hop into the elevator, which is lined with seats. The elevator doors close and the show begins. Up and down, the elevator chooses the floors for you. Each time they open, you are treated to a new scene. The story is fun and dramatic. But when you finally arrive at a floor where you can get out, it's time to explore.

Lead your grandchild to the top and to the spectacular overlook, where he can see across the river to the Pillsbury mill. He'll also have a wonderful view of the locks and St. Anthony Falls, the Stone Arch Bridge and the Mississippi River gorge.

Inside, the exhibits provide plenty of information, but there are three places sure to grab your grandkid's attention. The first is the kitchen. If you come on the right day, you and your grandchild can take part in cookie baking or other kitchen activities—all of which end with the best part: tasting.

The second big draw is a table with boats, trains, trucks and terrain. Imagination is put into play, and your grandchild can ship the grain by land, rail or water. Just around the corner is the water room. Here you can play with your grandchild as he learns about water flow, uses locks and dams, floats logs and boats, and engages in a wonderful set of unstructured experiments.

There are many more exhibits and places to explore at the Mill City Museum—far too many to describe here. Plan to spend at least four hours, but you may want to stay longer if your grandchild can't stop "milling" around.

Bonding and bridging:

Baking is one of those simple activities that a child views as a rite of passage. There's nothing quite like that first time in the kitchen, being old enough to help Mom, Dad, Grandpa or Grandma with the cake, cookies or bread. It can start with something as simple as applying the frosting. Next your grandchild can graduate to stirring the mix. Finally, he can begin adding the ingredients himself. It could get messy, and you may want to think twice about eating it—but, oh, what fun!

This is a special time, one in which your grandchild learns that he can do things himself. It's his first step on a path toward achievement and independence. He'll be happy that he took that step with you.

A word to the wise:

The elevator is a must. Step into that old freight elevator and seat yourself on one of the bleachers. Your grandchild and you will stop on all of the floors in a sequence that tells the story of the people who worked in the mills. You'll learn about the milling business and a sense of this place. Voices come through the speakers, lights take you through exhibits, and films play in the background. All combine to make you feel as though you're moving through an active mill.

Age of grandchild: 8 and up

Best season: All

Contact: Mill City Museum, 704 South Second Street, Minneapolis, MN 55401 • (612) 341-7555 • mcm@mnhs.org www.millcitymuseum.org

Also check out:

Marine Mill, Marine on St. Croix; (320) 532-5646; www.exploreminnesota.com/attractions/14278.html

Old Mill State Park, Argyle; (218) 437-8174; www.dnr.state.mn.us/state_parks/old_mill

Phelps Mill Park, Underwood; www.co.otter-tail.mn.us/phelpsmill

Now that I've reached the age where I need my children more than they need me, I really understand how grand it is to be a grandmother. Mrs. Margaret Whitlam

Minneapolis Sculpture Garden

The historical gateway to Minneapolis is through Loring Park. It is an area that brings together the spiritual, the natural and the commercial. Today there is a fourth element: aesthetics, which is well represented by the Minneapolis Sculpture Garden.

If art showcases the highest form of imagination and expression, then we can celebrate the fact that this glorious eleven-acre park features form, texture and

a sense of humor. "Spoonbridge and Cherry" has become a symbol of the city and can be found on postcards and brochures wherever Minneapolis is promoted. It is a fountain, a whimsical arrow pointing to the city center and a nod to the cereal history of General Mills and Pillsbury—all of that and a cherry on top!

There is so much more to see at the Sculpture Garden, and your grandchild's imagination will run wild. The Irene Hixon Whitney Bridge crosses Hennepin Avenue and seems to reverse itself, as though debating whether to come, go or just stay where it is. The bridge also connects the Sculpture Garden with Loring Park's mix of groomed, wild and designed landscapes.

The vine-covered arbor and flower garden is another gorgeous attraction. The beautiful display of brightly colored flowers is sure to attract your grandchild's attention. She'll also enjoy the sculpture pad, which offers unique shapes and a chance for your grandchild to interpret what she sees, as well as the outdoor galleries, which feature plenty of diverse creations.

If it is raining or too cold outside, the greenhouse's glass conservatory is home to Frank Gehry's Standing Glass Fish. Here, your grandchild and you will find palm trees and flowers providing a soft, colored background for the enormous fish that rises from a pool. The combination of live palms and glass fish is a mix of Minnesota's fishing heritage and the winter destinations of our snowbirds.

When you put it all together, you get the largest urban Sculpture Garden in the world and a can't-miss site for sharing the best of Minnesota with your grandchild.

Bonding and bridging:

The Sculpture Garden is a great place to explore our perceptions. The many playful, colorful, imaginative objects are wonderful creations. But no one truly sees what the artist saw, and no one sees what the person next to her does. The lines, the contrasts and the imagery are open to interpretation, and therefore, seeing these sculptures with someone else helps us to discover our own understandings. Ask your grandchild to share her perceptions of the art with you. Then share your own with her. She may be surprised that your view differs from her own, but that's okay. Just be prepared to explain why you see what you do.

Our experiences and influences shade our points of view outside the Sculpture Garden, as well as in. An exercise in perceptions will help both of you to realize this. After all, just because someone disagrees with you doesn't mean that either of you is wrong.

A word to the wise:

A walk across the Irene Hixon Whitney Bridge is a wonderful trek. The stark contrast between the quiet of the park and the hectic pace of the roadway is quite a sensory experience, and the difference between the Sculpture Garden and the more natural park is another fun comparison. When you and your grandchild pass the spot where the pastels shift from yellow to blue, you'll both experience physical and visual sensations that lead to an even deeper appreciation of the design.

Age of grandchild: All

Best season: Summer

Contact: Minneapolis Sculpture Garden, 726 Vineland Place
Minneapolis, MN 55403 • (612) 370-4929 • http://garden.walkerart.org

Also check out:

Caponi Art Park, Eagan; (651) 454-9412; www.caponiartpark.org

Franconia Sculpture Park, Shafer; (651) 465-3701; www.franconia.org

The closest friends I have made all through life have been people who also grew up close to a loved and living grandmother or grandfather. MARGARET MEAD

Metris Uptown Art Fair

Uptown is a trendy zone in South Minneapolis, filled with restaurants, bookstores and theaters. It is also the site for one of the best art festivals in the region: the Metris Uptown Art Fair. Hennepin Avenue is blocked off to cars, and booths are set up along the road to display some of the region's best creativity.

Since 1963, when the Uptown Art Fair started as the dream of three businessmen, the event has grown to become the ninth largest in the country. It attracts more than 375 artists and 350,000 visitors each year.

The Uptown Art Fair can take days to wander through—if you truly want to see everything. However that's not the goal for your grandchild. For him, this trip is about being exposed to art. It needs to be done in a gentle way and in a limited amount of time.

Casually lead your grandchild through the maze of artwork. Show him examples from every medium: paint, sculpture, drawing, photography, jewelry, you name it. Some of the art is very serious, some abstract and some just plain fun. Not all of it will be appealing to him but the rush of people and the mass of creativity will help him to understand that art is important to everyone, that it has a value and that there are many forms of expression.

In 1985 the festival began requiring its artists to submit their work to be judged. The results of this decision can still be seen today: The quality of artwork is amazing to behold. At times, the place can become an overload of stimulus, but the fact that a crowd of this size gathers for such a positive event is very encouraging.

While you're visiting, plan to eat some of the delicious food. There is plenty to choose from; food tents are available near the YMCA and the mall.

It is important that we recognize children as the art patrons of tomorrow. The Uptown Art Fair does just that. Students and teachers from local schools collaborate to create pieces of art, and the fair also offers a kids' activity center—making this the perfect place to introduce your grandchild to the beauty of art.

Bonding and bridging:

Why do we have art? Why is it important? For the answer, look no further than your own grandchild. Children are drawn to and inspired by art. They see something that sparks their imagination, and off they go into their own world of play and creativity.

At the Metris Uptown Art Fair, let your grandchild look closely. Let him meet an artist and create a perspective on art. When you get home, have your grandchild create some art of his own. Encourage him to be creative, and help him find the materials to express his own ideas. When he's finished, ask why he created what he did. Was he "inspired" by the art at the fair? Did seeing another artist's work give him ideas of his own? How does art make him feel? These questions are the keys to opening your grandchild's eyes about the role of art in our society.

A word to the wise:

The Metris Uptown Art Fair has many creative and wonderful booths, but be sure to take your grandchild to see Tomorrow's Stars Seen Today Art Fair. This is the youth art fair within the larger celebration. If you have a grandchild with real talent for art, you might even want to encourage him to enter. However, the most important thing for your grandchild is to see that there is potential for all ages in the field of art.

Age of grandchild: 10 and up

Best season: August (usually the first weekend)

Contact: Uptown Association, 1406 West Lake Street, Suite 202, Minneapolis, MN 55408 • (612) 823-4581
info@uptownminneapolis.com • www.uptownminneapolis.com/art-fair/

Also check out:

Bemidji community art fairs, Bemidji; www.bcac-mn.org/Artfairs.html

Loring Park Art Festival (held in conjunction with the Uptown Art Fair), Minneapolis; www.loringparkartfestival.com

Powderhorn Art Fair (held in conjunction with the Uptown Art Fair), Minneapolis; www.powderhornartfair.com

One of the most powerful handclasps is that of a new grandbaby around the finger of a grandfather. Joy Hargrove

The Bakken
Library and Museum

Well hidden from the general public, looking like an ancient mausoleum at its entrance, a lightning bolt streaking down the welcome sign—what is this place? The Bakken Library and Museum is a celebration of electricity, and it honors the way that electricity saves and contributes to life.

Before your grandchild has a chance to say, "Museums are boring," she'll be transfixed by the Frankenstein exhibit inside. From there she is hooked, thirsting for more knowledge at every turn. For instance, it was common in author Mary Shelley's time for electricity to be used to help restore life to drowning victims. It was also the time when Luigi Galvani applied electricity to frogs' legs and saw "life" take shape in the muscular reactions (the kicking legs). Suddenly "galvanizing" became a new word, and the newspaper wags wondered if someone could galvanize a corpse.

At the Bakken Museum, your grandchild and you are given a chance to see how medicine has used electricity, how our basic understanding of electricity has changed and how we continue to find new ways to use electricity.

The museum inhabits the home of Earl E. Bakken, inventor of the transistorized cardiac pacemaker. It combines an eclectic—as well as electric—mix of architecture and science. The mission of the museum is to share the benefits and understanding of electricity and magnetism in life, science and society.

Your grandchild will be impressed by the Bakken's extensive library, classes and camps for kids, and a wonderful collection of displays—including 2,500 machines that harness electricity for human use. Some are pretty strange and entertaining, such as the Electrarium, which creates sound waves as the musician disrupts electrical currents in the air between antennae.

Visiting the museum may be a "trip down memory lane" for you, but that makes it even more interesting for your grandchild. You can share your own experiences with (and without) electricity, and she may be amazed to learn that you didn't have a cell phone or a computer when you were her age. All of this makes the Bakken a fun and interesting place for an intergenerational visit.

Bonding and bridging:

It's amazing how quickly the world changes, and the Bakken is the perfect place to exemplify this. Look at how electricity has altered our lives in the past fifty years. As we get older, it is human nature to resist this. We tend to get set in our ways. But it is important for our grandchildren to understand that change is a part of life, and they must be able to adapt to it.

Tell your grandchild what life was like for you as a child: the things that you had and the things that you didn't have. Ask her to imagine living back then and how different life would be. Have her count how many times she uses electricity in a day. She'll likely be surprised at how much she takes for granted. Next, ask her what she thinks will be different when she has grandchildren some day. By dreaming about change and advances in technology, your grandchild will be better equipped to adapt when change occurs.

A word to the wise:

For hands-on experiments, don't miss Science Saturdays! These are not lectures. Instead, you and your grandchild might build a skeetball machine, find your way through a laser maze or create your own magnet game. This is fun for the child and for you, and it is another wonderful exposure to the potential of science.

Age of grandchild: 10 and up

Best season: All

Contact: The Bakken Library and Museum, 3537 Zenith Avenue South, Minneapolis, MN 55416 • (612) 926-3878
information@thebakken.org • www.thebakken.org

Also check out:

Bell Museum of Natural History, Minneapolis; (612) 624-7083; www.bellmuseum.org

Headwaters Center, Bemidji; (218) 444-4472; www.hscbemidji.org

Science Museum of Minnesota, St. Paul; (800) 221-9444; www.smm.org

Family faces are magic mirrors. Looking at people who belong to us, we see the past, present and future. GAIL LUMET BUCKLEY

49

Lyndale Park Gardens

Green is the color we miss most during winter, so we spend an inordinate amount of time working on our lawns and gardens throughout the warm months. We love nature's greens. That's why Lyndale Park Gardens is a perfect place to bring our grandchildren.

No other Minnesota destination does a better job of bringing together the elements of nature and humankind than the parks adjacent to Lake Harriet. Lyndale Park Gardens encompasses three main sections: the wild landscape of the Thomas Sadler Roberts Bird Sanctuary, the Rose Garden and the Peace Rock Garden.

The Roberts Bird Sanctuary opens the season. Natural spring ephemerals bloom on the forest floor, and flying flowers (otherwise known as warblers) fill the air. Your grandchild will be astounded by the colorful mix of birds—found in the middle of the city! The trail truly feels like a walk in the woods.

The Rose Garden is the second-oldest of its kind in the United States. Its breathtaking planting arrangement has not changed since it opened in 1908.

You and your grandchild will find more than three thousand roses (250 kinds) and sixty thousand flowers in bloom at the peak of growing season. The spicy scent fills the air and will have the two of you talking about it for days.

Across the street, you'll find the newer Lyndale Park Peace Rock Garden, which opened in 1983. Together you can examine rocks from Hiroshima and Nagasaki, Japan. Plus you'll appreciate the quiet waterfall, the subtle rock sculptures and the many opportunities for Zen contemplation. The Rock Garden is a one-of-a-kind combination of art and garden, with a very powerful message for the world: It is a reminder of the choice to become a warrior or a peacemaker.

From the sculptured fountains to the mowed hills beneath majestic oaks, people come to this area to seek a variety of pleasures. Bring blankets to sit on and books to read, or enjoy a friendly game of catch. Lyndale Park Gardens is a convergence of tranquility, energy and fun.

Bonding and bridging:

Perhaps the most powerfully moving location in Lyndale Park Gardens is the Lyndale Park Peace Rock Garden—more specifically, the rocks from Hiroshima and Nagasaki, Japan. Few exhibits are more stark reminders of the horrors and tragedies of war.

Talk to your grandchild about war. Ask him what he thinks is the purpose of war. Why do we fight? How can we build a peaceful world? You may want to bring the discussion closer to home—about fighting with siblings or with classmates at school. Regardless, the message is simple and clear: Violence is not the solution. Help your grandchild to realize this, and you'll help him become a better person, one who always looks for peaceful answers.

A word to the wise:

In August, children hang origami paper cranes on the park's trees and shrubs in honor of Sadako Sasaki, a child who died of radiation sickness ten years after the bombing of Hiroshima. The young girl believed in a legend that anyone who folded a thousand cranes was granted a wish. Now, in this small park in Minnesota, your grandchild can find a connection to that event and to the world, by hanging an origami paper crane representing a plea for peace.

Age of grandchild: All

Best season: Late spring and early summer

Contact: Minneapolis Park & Recreation Board,
1500 East Lake Harriet Parkway, Minneapolis, MN 55409
(612) 230-6400 • www.minneapolisparks.org

Also check out:

August Schell Brewery Gardens, New Ulm; (800) 770-5020; www.schellsbrewery.com/brew_tour_thegardens.php

Clemens Rose Garden, St. Cloud; (320) 255-7216 (Parks Department); www.munsingerclemens.com

Cowling Arboretum, Northfield; (507) 646-5413; http://apps.carleton.edu/campus/arb/

Como Park Zoo
and Conservatory

The barking of Sparky the Seal and the overwhelming smells of the cathouse are some of my strongest childhood memories of the Como Park Zoo and Conservatory. I also think fondly of riding the miniature train and the merry-go-round in the zoo's amusement park. Today, the Como Park Zoo and Conservatory remains as captivating to our grandchildren as it was to us so many years ago.

Even as a child I sensed the unfairness of keeping a full-grown tiger in a small, concrete cell. Fortunately the zoo, the conservatory and the amusement park

have all been upgraded. The animals live in more suitable enclosures. The cats and primates have access to outdoor areas with fresh air and grass. The zoo's overall appearance and feeling is much happier and much more humane.

The Conservatory is still a lush, humid, green oasis, but nowadays it is more closely connected to the zoo experience with a clean, comfortable dining area and gift store. It seems natural to move from one part to the next.

The pathways, both indoors and out, are easy to negotiate—even with a stroller. Plus the zoo area is compact enough that you won't feel exhausted after touring all of the exhibits. Be sure to tell your grandchild how different it was when you came to the zoo as a child and what your favorite animal was then and now.

Discuss each of the magnificent creatures you see; use this opportunity—when the animals have your grandchild's curiosity running wild—to pass on a little knowledge.

During the summer season, be prepared to hear, "Can we please go on some rides?" What child can resist the excitement of spinning and racing around a circular track? I know I couldn't. Lastly, if you really want to cement the memories of the visit, let your grandchild choose an edible treat from one of the various stands.

The Como Park Zoo and Conservatory has come a long way since its start in the late 1800s. It has entered the twenty-first century with a much more focused message of preserving planetary biodiversity.

Bonding and bridging:

Respect for life is a hard topic to cover in almost any situation, but the Como Park Zoo and Conservatory provides a wonderful setting for discussing plants and animals.

What are the animals' purpose in being captive? Is it right? What do they need to exist? Could they survive in Minnesota on their own? What is the difference between a pet and a zoo animal? How can we enjoy and respect animals and plants? What is our obligation to other forms of life? These are big questions without simple answers. But a place like this is the right setting to start a child on a lifetime of searching for the right answers.

A word to the wise:

The Sparky the Seal show was entertaining when I was a kid, and it still has children laughing today. The show is used to teach kids important lessons, rather than simply amusing them. The show provides an excellent learning opportunity for your grandchild and for you.

Age of grandchild: All

Best season: Spring (when the baby animals are born)

Contact: Como Park Zoo and Conservatory, 1225 Estabrook Drive, St. Paul, MN 55103 • (651) 487-8200 • www.comozooconservatory.org

Also check out:

Lake Superior Zoo, Duluth; (218) 730-4900; www.lszoo.org

Minnesota Zoo, Apple Valley; (800) 366-7811, www.mnzoo.org

Minnesota History Center

History is an aspect of this book that pops up time and again. Why? Because studying and celebrating history is an important step toward understanding ourselves. Fortunately, teaching our grandchildren about Minnesota history is not a difficult task; there is evidence of this great state's past all around us. To make our task even easier, the Minnesota History Center has collected much of this evidence and presents it in a fascinating, entertaining environment.

As the apex for historical study, the History Center is a complicated building. Many people come just to eat the wonderful lunches and to sit outside on summer afternoons. Others come for the library, where our most complete historical documents can be found in a modern and accessible system. However, most come to enjoy the complex exhibit center where hands-on is the rule—and that is most certainly why you should bring your grandchild with you.

Explore the center. Interpreters are available to help explain the exhibits, and your grandchild will love the revolving displays which are three-dimensional

and very inviting. Large railroad cars, storefronts, a record studio and a variety of Minnesota memorabilia are just some of the things you and your grandchild will come across.

You should also make time for your grandchild to enjoy a historical play in the People's Theatre. And a stop in the historical library is another supplement to your grandchild's visit. Research a project on a topic that would be of interest to both of you—perhaps about your neighborhood, a place where you worked, a relative who achieved some notoriety or your old school. Set out to discover something, and you will also learn about the library, how it works, what is available and how to access it.

Most of all, your day at the Minnesota History Center is about discovering the past. Keep it light-hearted and fun, and your grandchild may develop a deeper interest in this most interesting of subjects.

Bonding and bridging:

We all have different ways that we prefer to learn. Some people would rather listen to instructions, while others need to see it done. For children, the hands-on approach is almost always a great method. At the Minnesota History Center, learning hands-on is what the experience is all about.

Empower your grandchild. Encourage her curiosity, and allow her to explore all that the History Center has to offer. By providing her with an opportunity to experience how the center looks, sounds, smells and feels, you are building within her a foundation for discovery—both of herself and of the world around her.

A word to the wise:

The Minnesota History Center's exhibits change regularly, and special classes that bring history to life are frequently offered. You can add to your visit with a stroll to the James J. Hill House, the Cathedral of St. Paul and the State Capitol. All are connected by sidewalks and are an easy walking distance from the center. The combination is one of history and history in the making.

Age of grandchild: 6 and up

Best season: All

Contact: Minnesota History Center, 345 Kellogg Boulevard West,
St. Paul, MN 55102 • (888) 727-8386 • www.mnhs.org/historycenter

Also check out:

Charles Lindbergh House and History Center, Little Falls; (320) 616-5421; www.mnhs.org/places/sites/lh

Northeast Minnesota History Center (University of Minnesota), Duluth; (218) 726-8526; www.d.umn.edu/lib/nemhc

Northwest Minnesota Historical Center, Moorhead; (218) 477-2346; www.mnstate.edu/archives

Southwest Regional History Center, Marshall; (507) 537-7373; www.southwestmsu.edu/history_center

If I had known how wonderful it would be to have grandchildren, I'd have had them first. Lois Wyse

Saints
Baseball Game

Baseball is America's pastime for a reason. It's not the most action-packed, exciting sport, but most games are full of tense moments. The game of baseball is about anticipation. The odds are against the batter on every pitch, yet these tremendous athletes manage to hit, run and score—bringing eager fans to their feet.

For Minnesotans, Midway Stadium is a treasure. You can't beat the painted, dolled up, outdoor environment in the middle of St. Paul. What could be better than a warm summer night, a wonderfully manicured diamond, a modern scoreboard and cheering on our Saints?

Win or lose, the team is always entertaining. These players are good, they are enthusiastic, and they play—not for millions of dollars—but for wages that most fans can relate to. Best of all they play for the love of the game, giving an honest, all-out effort on every pitch.

Adding to the mix, trains rumble behind the stadium walls. Grandparents can get a massage from a nun while watching the game. There is also an opportunity to get a haircut, to root for a pig that wears a tutu and to enjoy a variety of hokey promotions, games and activities.

If there are more errors and less gloss, so be it. We can cheer and go home feeling good, no matter the game's results. The team and the players have connections to the local area, and every once in a while an old pro will don the uniform to try and prove that there is still good baseball in his body. We all like to see the effort that these men give.

An afternoon or evening at a Saints baseball game brings back memories of my family's old backyard, playing catch with my grandfather, who was most definitely old school. He called curve balls "in pitches," and screwballs were "out pitches." We would pace off a reasonable distance then let fly with a combination of tosses, conversation and kidding.

Bringing your grandchild to a game is a chance to enjoy American tradition, to reminisce and to have a good time.

Bonding and bridging:

We've all heard the old saying, "Practice makes perfect." There is no better example of this than a baseball player. It's no easy task to pitch a strike, and it is even harder to hit a baseball that's traveling more than ninety miles per hour. Each of these athletes has spent and continues to spend several hours a day practicing, practicing, practicing. They have all dedicated themselves to success.

What does your grandchild wish he were better at? Maybe it's a sport or an activity such as playing the piano. Maybe he hopes to be a writer one day. Ask him to think about what he's doing now to improve his skills. Help him create a practice plan. If you can, make yourself a part of his plan. Shoot hoops with him every Saturday, or assist him with his homework. If nothing else, check in with him every so often to see if he's sticking to it. Having someone to guide him will keep him on track, and he will learn that hard work and dedication pay off over time.

A word to the wise:

Come early and tailgate. A Saints game is a fun venue with casual picnics and activities. Plenty of children and their families participate, especially before the last game of the regular season, and the combination creates an excellent social environment. The Saints also have birthday parties for kids that include a Saints general admission ticket, a voucher for a hot dog, popcorn, peanuts and soda, two vouchers for the kids' zone games and a free Saints T-shirt, as well as a special birthday message on the video board during the game.

Age of grandchild: 8 and up

Best season: Summer

Contact: St. Paul Saints, 1771 Energy Park Drive,
St. Paul, MN 55108 • (651) 644-6659 • www.saintsbaseball.com

Also check out:

Brainerd Blue Thunder; (218) 828-2825; www.brainerdbluethunder.com

Fargo-Moorhead Redhawks; (800) 303-6161; www.fmredhawks.com

Rochester Honkers; (507) 289-1170; www.rochesterhonkers.com

Twin City Model Railroad Museum

How many of us grandparents had an electric train set to play with when we were kids? Think of the countless hours of joy we received from playing with those revolutionary toys. Nowadays, toys come with all sorts of bells and whistles, but it was those old train sets that captured our imaginations. We can share our childhood railroading fascinations with our grandchildren, during a visit to the Twin City Model Railroad Museum.

Established in 1939, the Model Railroad Museum is an extension of the Model Railroad Club. Its location in Bandana Square (St. Paul), a site that has some railroad history, adds to the experience. Old railroad buildings and an old railroad engine mark your location as you drive into the parking lot—a very nice touch.

The museum's volunteers have gone to great lengths to create a landscape and a cityscape that are authentic and scaled to the trains. Plus, the trains are historic in themselves, representing such railroads as Twin Cities Hiawatha, the North Coast Limited, the Zephyrs, the Black Hawk, the Empire Builder and even the original "400."

The model's accuracy is extraordinary. Show your grandchild the St. Anthony Falls area, including details such as the Stone Arch Bridge and the old milling district. You can also point out the Great Northern Depot, the trolley system and the scenic bluff country along the Mississippi in southeastern Minnesota.

On the walls around the exhibit you'll find old travel posters, and often a club member or a railroad enthusiast can be found. If asked, they are always more than willing to add details to what you're seeing.

The golden era of railroads may be gone, but this miniaturization is the best representation of those days that you can find anywhere in Minnesota. I think you'll agree that there is something absolutely hypnotic about seeing the movement, the color and the scenery. It almost feels real—for you and for your grandchild. The Model Railroad Museum just might have your grandchild wishing for an electric train set of her own.

Bonding and bridging:

Regardless of whether your grandchild has any interest in models or railroads, the Model Railroad Museum is worth a visit. Of course, the history it presents is fascinating, but there is also something to be said about celebrating a craft done well. These miniaturizations are so meticulously created that you can't help but be awestruck by them.

This, then, is an opportunity for a lesson worth learning. Teach your grandchild to celebrate a job well done. Almost everyone discovers (or chooses) a skill that she can do exceptionally well—whether it's hitting a baseball or putting together model trains. If we demonstrate the behavior of appreciating and acknowledging the greatness in others, our grandchildren can't help but do the same.

A word to the wise:

There are model railroad clubs in the Twin Cities, Rochester, Monticello, Winona, St. James and Duluth. If your grandchild is captivated with trains, connect her with one of these groups. However, before you invest in expensive electric train sets for her, make sure that she's ready. Start with a wooden set. No batteries or electricity are required; these trains run on imagination.

Age of grandchild: All

Best season: All

Contact: Twin City Model Railroad Museum,
1021 Bandana Boulevard East, Suite 222, Saint Paul, MN 55108
(651) 647-9628 • tcmrm@tcmrm.org • www.tcmrm.org

Also check out:

End-O-Line Railroad Park & Museum, Currie; (507) 763-3708; www.endoline.com

Lake Superior Railroad Museum, Duluth; (218) 733-7519; www.lsrm.org

Minnehaha Depot at Minnehaha Park, Minneapolis; (651) 228-0263; www.mnhs.org/places/sites/md

Minnesota Transportation Museum: Jackson Street Roundhouse, St. Paul; (651) 228-0263, Extension. 3105; www.mtmuseum.org

A child needs a grandparent, anybody's grandparent, to grow a little more securely into an unfamiliar world. CHARLES AND ANN MORSE

State Capitol

We are a culture of symbols, and few structures are more symbolic than the State Capitol. The building, which opened on January 2, 1905, stands on a slight hill that slopes downward toward the city and across from the Cathedral of St. Paul.

Modeled after the U.S. Capitol, this structure is unique and awe-inspiring. It should be seen from both inside and outside to get a sense of its timelessness. Walk your grandchild up the central mall through the parkland and statuary. Pay homage to a couple of statues and discuss how people have used these common grounds for protests, rallies and demonstrations and how those acts are the basis for democracy. Let your grandchild know that this is his Capitol. The people in it are his representatives, and the right to assemble and disagree is at the heart of what America is— from the Boston Tea Party to today.

Point out the gold-leafed copper and steel statue near the top of the building. Called "Progress of the State," this symbol should remind us of our state's tie to nature and our need to keep Minnesota clean, green and protected for future generations. The four horses refer to the power of the earth, wind, fire and water. The women in the statue represent civilization; the man represents prosperity.

Next, lead your grandchild inside. The building is imposing with its high ceilings, atmospheric lighting, artwork depicting past governors and other historical scenes lit by individual lamps. The rotunda feels like a place where great ideas should be discussed, and the Georgia marble takes the sunlight from the dome, giving a mystical hue to the central circle. This may be the single most impressive spot in the Capitol.

Look into the chambers where laws are passed. Go into the galleries if the Senate is in session, and watch the messy process from the balcony. Stroll the halls and find your senator, then move next door to find your representative.

You are welcome to wander on your own, but the Historical Society provides regular tours. (The desk is to the right of the main entrance.) If you've never been to the State Capitol before, this is a good way to get started.

Bonding and bridging:

All of us can make a difference in this country, and the State Capitol is the place to let grandchildren know it. The building is, in essence, ours. These are our employees, and it is our responsibility to make sure that they are doing a good job. If they aren't, we vote them out.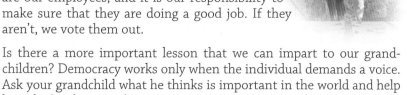

Is there a more important lesson that we can impart to our grandchildren? Democracy works only when the individual demands a voice. Ask your grandchild what he thinks is important in the world and help him draft a letter to his senator or representative. Show him how to participate in the institution of government.

This is a place to begin teaching your grandchild that he has a voice and that he should use it to stand up for what he believes in.

A word to the wise:

Make an appointment to visit your senator and representative. Even if you know them at home, they look different in their offices. Get a photo taken. Be prepared with a few good questions so the conversation doesn't lag, but do not make this a lobbying visit.

Age of grandchild: 12 and up

Best season: Winter (when senators and representatives are in session)

Contact: State Capitol, 75 Dr. Martin Luther King Boulevard, St. Paul, MN 55155 • (651) 296-2881 • statecapitol@mnhs.org
www.mnhs.org/places/sites/msc

Also check out:

County courthouses (visit one near you);
www.mnpreservation.org/portfolio.MN_Courthouse_Photos.php

Minneapolis City Hall, Minneapolis;
www.ci.minneapolis.mn.us/government

Rochester City Hall, Rochester; www.ci.rochester.mn.us

St. Paul City Hall, St. Paul; www.stpaul.gov/leisure/cityhall

My grandfather was a giant of a man...When he walked, the earth shook. When he laughed, the birds fell out of the trees. His hair caught fire from the sun. His eyes were patches of sky. ETH CLIFFORD, *THE REMEMBERING BOX*

Minnesota Children's Museum

Is this a museum or a playground? Does it matter? To the kids there is no question about what the Minnesota Children's Museum is: a place for them. The four floors of creativity include colors, designs and educational content interwoven into one of the most child-engaging places in the state. Your job is to guide your grandchild, but let her lead the way.

Keep an eye on safety, namely the possible conflicts that can arise from lots of little hands and feet concentrating on the objects that have grabbed their attention (and not on each other). To help, volunteers roam the facility and provide inspiration and control without being imposing. As a result, you can let your grandchild's imagination run wild; just try not to let her run out of sight.

Pack a lunch or some snacks. (You'll find no healthy food options inside.) If you bring a stroller, check it on the first floor. Then walk or ride the elevator to the fourth floor, and take your time working your way down.

The Habitot gallery on the fourth floor is perfect for young children. It is safe, age-restricted and filled with places to explore. On the opposite side of the building is the outdoor Rooftop ArtPark where older children can express themselves. Between the two, you'll find a discovery classroom with revolving displays and a wonderful Earth World gallery.

The third floor is for reading. There are plenty of changing rooms, bathrooms and places to sit, too. You will need them all before the end of a full day.

On the second floor, the Our World gallery is a life-sized community—a place for the child to explore a make-believe world of stores, homes and buses. And the World Works gallery is a collection of mechanical contraptions that indirectly teach about levers and pulleys, water flow, gravity and mechanical forces. It's so hands-on and imaginative that there is no need for explanations. Also on the second floor is the Atrium, a gathering place where jugglers, storytellers and educational entertainers provide laughs and knowledge.

The museum understands that the role of grandparents is essential. It offers a season pass for us at the same rate as the parents. That's a very good deal!

Bonding and bridging:

No one likes to be corrected—including grand-children. Fortunately, there are not any wrong answers at the Minnesota Children's Museum. The entire place is rich with activities waiting to be tried, and there isn't any one "right" way to play. Instead, the experience is about exploration and about children finding their own way.

For you, this is a chance to practice the art of stepping aside. Let your grandchild experiment with different methods of problem solving. Keep your suggestions to a minimum, and offer guidance only as a last resort. When she has completed the activity, challenge her creativity by asking, "How many other ways could you do that? Can you think of a different solution?"

By doing so, you will be sending your grandchild a message that there isn't always just one answer, and it's okay to make mistakes as long as you learn from them.

A word to the wise:

This is your day to enable and observe. Take advantage of the Curiosity Center. Here the museum staff helps children make creative objects using art, focusing their creative energies. The center is a good "slow-down" place that still engages the child. Later in the day, when you begin to feel tired, take her to the Book Nook to relax with you, so she can stay a little longer.

Age of grandchild: Nine months to 10 years

Best season: All

Contact: Minnesota Children's Museum, 10 West Seventh Street, St. Paul, MN 55102 • (651) 225-6000 • mcm@mcm.org • www.MCM.org

Also check out:

Children's Discovery Museum, Grand Rapids; (218) 326-1900; www.cdmkids.org

Duluth Children's Museum, Duluth; (218) 733-7543; www.duluthchildrensmuseum.org

At age seven, children have as passionate a longing for creative interactions and learning as they earlier had for explorations of the world. Joseph Chilton Pearce, *The Magical Child*

Science Museum of Minnesota

Science isn't the favorite subject of a lot of children. For some it's considered a very dry, boring topic. Thank goodness we have the Science Museum of Minnesota! Inside, grandparents and grandchildren alike can see learning come alive. If for no other reason, that makes a trip to the Science Museum a worthwhile thing to do.

The Science Museum of Minnesota can trace its roots to 1906 when a group of businessmen met to discuss "the intellectual and the scientific growth of St. Paul." What began as the St. Paul Institute of Science and Letters soon became the Science Museum of Minnesota.

The museum is located next to the Mississippi River in St. Paul's growing, vital riverfront area. It's built into the bluff, connecting science with nature. When you're inside the museum, you'll find some interesting displays related to the great river. Plus, the best part is that the displays are strategically placed, so you can gaze at the Mississippi River through the windows beyond them—a most effective supplement to the museum experience.

In total, the site offers 370,000 square feet and countless exhibits about the human body, dinosaurs, fossils and several other fascinating subjects. The Experiment Gallery is a favorite stop. The hands-on environment makes learning fun. Your grandchild can create a weather system, operate a steam engine and watch a tornado form!

In the Collections Gallery, your grandchild will encounter an Egyptian mummy and a two-headed turtle. You may also want to plan some extra time to watch a movie in the William L. McKnight-3M Omnitheater. Most kids enjoy movies, and this place has the largest permanently installed projector in the world! The movies shown are interesting, entertaining and informative. (You don't have to tell your grandchild that he's learning!)

A trip to the Science Museum of Minnesota is a chance to learn, to bond and to have fun. The possibilities here are endless, and who knows? Maybe science will become your grandchild's favorite subject.

Bonding and bridging:

The most special thing about the Science Museum of Minnesota is that it makes learning fun. This isn't about reading textbooks or memorizing complicated formulas; it's about seeing science in action and being a part of the scientific process.

Any time you can make learning an enjoyable experience for your grandchild, you must seize the opportunity. A child who has fun learning is a child who seeks greater knowledge. And as he continues to get smarter, he might discover that those textbooks and complicated formulas are quite fascinating too.

A word to the wise:

The Science Live programs provide you with a wonderful way to engage and share science with your grandchild. Each event combines theater, science and interactive learning to create a long-lasting educational experience.

Age of grandchild: All

Best season: All

Contact: Science Museum of Minnesota, 120 West Kellogg Boulevard, St. Paul, MN 55102 • (800) 221-9444 • info@smm.org • www.smm.org

Also check out:

Bakken Library and Museum, Minneapolis; (612) 926-3878; www.thebakken.org

Bell Museum of Natural History, Minneapolis; (612) 624-7083; www.bellmuseum.org

Headwaters Center, Bemidji; (218) 444-4472; www.hscbemidji.org

Minnehaha Falls

The Grand Rounds National Scenic Byway encompasses several of the most enchanting spots in the Twin Cities. It's an amazing experience to see all of the sights as you hike, bike, paddle or drive. However, there's one location that's not only worth stopping for, it merits a visit all its own: Minnehaha Falls.

It's not the highest or the widest waterfall you'll come across in your travels. In fact, in 1848 artist Henry Lewis referred to Minnehaha Falls as "Little Falls." However, it may very well be the most beautiful in the state.

The sight is enchanting. Water flows from the rocky, green ledge, splashing into the pool below. The air around you is thick with mist, and the booming noise of water against water offers a comfort that cannot be described. It's awe-inspiring and it's wonderful.

Minnehaha Falls is related to St. Anthony Falls. The entire system began in downtown St. Paul and slowly moved upstream as the rocks eroded beneath the falling water. When the falls reached the point where Minnehaha Creek joins the Mississippi River, the erosion divided into two parts. Two separate and spectacular falls were the result.

Minnehaha Falls (or "laughing waters" as it translates from Dakota) is fifty feet high. It is the focal point of Minnehaha Park adjacent to Fort Snelling State Park, the Mississippi River National Waterway and the Minnesota River Valley National Wildlife Refuge. It's a great place for a grandparent-grandchild visit.

The park is a prominent city getaway that's set on the banks of Minnehaha Creek. Plan a picnic there, or dine at one of the nearby cafés. After lunch, take a quiet stroll around the area and contemplate the park's beauty. This shared time together doesn't need to be about anything more than enjoying each other's company.

After a few hours at Minnehaha Falls, you and your grandchild will understand why Henry Wadsworth Longfellow immortalized it in his poem "The Song of Hiawatha." This is a place of beauty, magic and wonder that will leave you speechless.

Bonding and bridging:

We can learn a lot about ourselves by studying waterfalls. Just as it is true about people, no two waterfalls are alike. Granted, some may look very similar, but when you take a closer look at the details, you'll notice the countless different ways that the water breaks around the rocks, splashes as it hits the pool below and accents the landscape around it.

When it comes to waterfalls and people, teach your grandchild to look deeper. Do not let her be content with surface judgments. Encourage her to be patient, to take her time and to truly observe and understand before she reaches any conclusions. This will go a long way toward raising a grandchild who truly appreciates the beauty in all people, as well as in nature.

A word to the wise:

Visit the statue of Hiawatha carrying the maiden Minnehaha across the stream. It is located on a small island west of the footbridge. You might even want to carry a few lines of Longfellow's "Song of Hiawatha" in your pocket. Read it, and remember that you have one-upped the poet—he never visited the falls!

Age of grandchild: All

Best season: All

Contact: The Longfellow House Information Center,
4800 Minnehaha Avenue, Minneapolis, MN 55415
(612) 230-6520 • www.minneapolisparks.org/grandrounds

Also check out:

Gooseberry Falls, Two Harbors; (218) 834-3855;
www.dnr.state.mn.us/state_parks/gooseberry_falls

Minneopa Falls, Mankato; (507) 389-5464;
www.dnr.state.mn.us/state_parks/minneopa

The real mystery of life is not a problem to be solved, it is a reality to be experienced. J.J. Van der Leeuw

Mississippi National River and Recreation Area

What's the best-kept secret in the Twin Cities? That's easy: the Mississippi National River and Recreation Area! Here you'll find seventy-two miles of riverfront, protected by the National Park System. Its headquarters is in front of the Science Museum, and most people think it's a gift store. Who knew?

The magnificent waterfront stretches from Harriet Island in St. Paul to Nicollet Island in Minneapolis. It is part of the Grand Rounds National Scenic Byway, the Great River Road National Scenic Highway and the Mississippi Riverway Birding Trail. Everything converges here, including the outdoors and a zest for life.

Hike, walk or drive. You'll come across fountains and pathways, bridges and steamboats. Treat your grandchild to a restaurant at St. Anthony on the Main, walk across the Stone Arch Bridge, or ride the trolley. Explore the art along the walkway, and cross the large car bridges. Your grandchild will get a thrill from watching the many different boats go through St. Anthony Lock and Dam, and he can observe how the tallest lock on the entire river works.

You absolutely must take him down to the river bottoms beneath the Mississippi's only waterfall. Fish the waters, paint, draw and bird watch. Trek downstream and cross over to the main campus of the University of Minnesota, then cross back on the multilevel bridge that separates bikes and pedestrians from cars. Follow the trail along the river and across the bluff tops to Minnehaha Falls, and take another set of trails to Fort Snelling and the state park where the Minnesota and Mississippi rivers join.

Cross over to St. Paul and enjoy the overlook across from the fort. Walk to the Crosby Farm preserve and to downtown St. Paul, or journey to the river and come back past Hidden Falls. Finally, follow the parkway along the upper level of the gorge that was cut by the headward erosion of St. Anthony Falls.

This is a tremendous excursion that reveals the best of Minnesota's delicate balance between progress and the natural world. It is an experience well worth sharing with your grandchild.

Bonding and bridging:

One of my favorite places in Minnesota to visit is the Mississippi National River and Recreation Area. I love the diversity of experiences this area offers. From restaurants and bridges to trolleys, boats and wildlife—it's all there.

Ask your grandchild to name his favorite places to visit, and write them all down. Next, ask him what he believes makes each of these locations special. Plan a trip to some of the places on his list. By doing so, you're showing your grandchild that you value his opinion and that you are taking an interest in the things he enjoys. This is a valuable activity that can only strengthen your relationship. Plus, it's an excuse to spend more time together!

A word to the wise:

Take a boat through St. Anthony lock; it is one of the most amazing river experiences you can have. Enter this large area at a level where you can talk to the men working the lock just above your head. As the doors behind you close, you are confined to this cement swimming pool. Suddenly you find yourself staring at the massive door in front of you. You begin to slide downward, feeling small like a minnow. Your free ride ends forty-nine feet below, as water runs off the doors in front of you. It's time to paddle (or motor) to the next lock, just downstream.

Age of grandchild: All

Best season: Spring, summer and fall

Contact: National Park Service (Mississippi); www.nps.gov/miss

Also check out:

Mississippi Levee Park and Prairie Island, Winona; www.villageprofile.com/minnesota/winona/08parks/topic.html

Munsinger and Clemens Gardens, St. Cloud; www.munsingerclemens.com

Red River Trails, Moorhead; www.riverkeepers.org/php/projects.php

St. Croix Wild and Scenic River, Stillwater; www.nps.gov/sacn

There is no other door to knowledge than the door Nature opens. And there is no truth but the truth we discover in Nature. Luther Burbank

Historic Fort Snelling

Ten-hut! Look sharp as you make your way toward Minnesota's most historic military landmark. Visit Historic Fort Snelling for a glimpse at the frontier life of soldiers, civilians and American Indians.

The year is 1827. You and your grandchild just stepped off a Mississippi steamboat. You gaze at majestic Fort Snelling, perched high atop a bluff that overlooks the Mississippi and Minnesota rivers. As you stroll inside the fort's impressive walls, you are greeted by a costumed guide. You've just entered a time machine that has taken you back nearly two hundred years, and your grandchild is more than likely having the time of his life!

The sights and sounds of the past are all around you. Watch as the soldiers shoot their muskets, and plug your ears when they set off the booming cannon. Your grandchild and you can even take part in everyday fort activities such as mending clothes, smelling the stew and singing with the soldiers (while shouldering a musket, no less)! Enjoy the show as the costumed actors demonstrate crafts, perform skits and run military drills.

Lead your grandchild up the original round tower and its counterparts: the half moon battery, the pentagonal tower and the hexagonal tower. Then visit the Sutler store, where you can purchase versions of original 1827 goods, including spruce gum.

Beware the guardhouse—there may be a malcontent interred, and the guards take no fooling around. Along those same lines, the hospital is definitely not a place where grandkids would want to have surgery!

Next on the list is a visit to the Fort Snelling History Center, adjacent to the fort. This area offers informative films and fascinating exhibits. But don't stop there. Fort Snelling State Park is home to a number of beautiful hiking trails.

History is fun and interactive at Historic Fort Snelling. Playacting, touring, hiking and exploring are all rolled into one—making this a favorite stop for grandchildren and grandparents alike.

Bonding and bridging:

We're grandparents, and we may be old. But we're not *that* old. Historic Fort Snelling predates even us—a concept a younger grandchild may not understand.

Here, we are not the instructors. We take on the roles of students, just like our grandchildren. This is history, and we can all learn about it together. It's a perfect way to introduce your grandchild to the fact that you don't have all of the answers—no one does. Plus, when she sees that you are as eager to learn new things as she is, she'll realize that we never stop learning. After all, we're never too old to learn a new trick.

A word to the wise:

Civil War Weekend every August is an exciting time for you and your grand-child to visit Historic Fort Snelling. It's 1865, the war has been over for months, and our brave soldiers are finally coming home! The First Minnesota Volunteer Infantry, Incorporated, and countless reenactors swarm to the site, bringing a sense of excitement with them. There is truly no better aspect of war than when the fighting is finished.

Age of grandchild: 3 and up

Best season: Summer

Contact: Historic Fort Snelling, 200 Tower Avenue, St. Paul, MN 55111
(612) 726-1171 • ftsnelling@mnhs.org • www.mnhs.org/places/sites/hfs/ or www.nps.gov/miss/maps/model/fort.html

Also check out:

Fort Belmont Park, Jackson; (507) 847-3867 (Jackson Area Chamber of Commerce); www.jacksonmn.com/fort_belmont/fort_belmont.htm

Grand Army of the Republic Hall, Litchfield; (320) 693-8911 (Meeker County Historical Society); www.garminnesota.org

I don't intentionally spoil my grandkids. It's just that correcting them often takes more energy than I have left. GENE PERRET

Wood Lake
Nature Center

Richfield, a southern suburb of the Twin Cities, is a tapestry of busy shopping, intersections, freeways, condominiums and housing developments. Yet amid this hectic city lies one of the best marsh areas in the state. Wood Lake Nature Center is a 150-acre island of wilderness hidden within the concrete jungle.

The area was originally a shallow lake until the construction of Interstate 35 broke the hardpan beneath the soil, causing the lake to drain and creating a marshy land. At first the location was considered a prime place for a golf course, but there was another movement afoot, championed by families and schools: the nature center movement.

While Minneapolis was famous for parks and greenways, the suburbs had been built in a frenzy of construction—with parks hardly on the radar screen. The Richfield community recognized their need and created a referendum. The people spoke, and Wood Lake was saved. The result is a place where people and nature come together.

Wood Lake Nature Center is a spot where your grandkids can view a live video cam that peeks into a bird's nest, can watch birds at a feeder and can check out the exhibits. It is a place where schools come for environmental studies and where families come to walk, participate in public programs and have birthday parties. The park is there for exercise of mind and spirit, and the center's special programs reflect that combination.

Bring your grandchild to Wood Lake Nature Center for some casual walking and lots of bird-viewing opportunities. Be sure to have him bring his camera, or perhaps you'll want to buy him a disposable camera for this occasion. Either way, the two of you will come across plenty of chances to take wonderful, close-up bird photographs.

Spend a few hours exploring and taking pictures, then go and get those snapshots developed. The two of you can "ooh" and "ahh" about your grandchild's photography skills. It's a perfect end to a day in which your grandchild grew a little closer to nature.

Bonding and bridging:

For children growing up in a big city, nature is not often at the forefront of their thoughts. They tend to develop a distance from the world that we all depend on for survival. Wood Lake Nature Center provides a solution. It allows kids to see the environment in the midst of the noise, the traffic and the shopping centers.

As grandparents, we must teach our grandchildren to maintain a connection with the natural world. We must help them find ways to blend human needs with the needs of our planet. The issues that we all face include urban development, pollution and competing interests. Explore with your grandchild some of these important and difficult issues. The nature center is an excellent example of what we can do to create a positive solution.

A word to the wise:

Come during spring. The flowers bloom, and the birds return. The land is vibrant and the experiences of color, movement, sound and scent cannot be topped. You should also sign up for a wild food session. Adding taste and texture to the experience will give your grandchild another conversation topic for the trip home.

Age of grandchild: All

Best season: Spring

Contact: Wood Lake Nature Center, 6710 Lake Shore Drive, Richfield, MN 55423 • (612) 861-9365 • www.woodlakenaturecenter.org

Also check out:

Hartley Nature Center, Duluth; (218) 724-6735; www.hartleynature.org

Paul Bunyan Nature Learning Center, Brainerd; (218) 829-9620

River Bend Nature Center, Faribault; (507) 332-7151; www.rbnc.org

Science Center at Maltby Nature Preserve, Randolph; (507) 664-0770; http://thesciencecentermnp.org

How beautifully the leaves grow old. How full of light and color are their last days. JOHN BURROUGHS

Minnesota Zoo

What kid doesn't enjoy going to the zoo? Even as adults we can find great pleasure in viewing the wild's most amazing animals. I was lucky enough to work at the Minnesota Zoo for nine years, and I have seen first-hand the joy that visiting the Minnesota Zoo can bring.

The zoo is located five miles south of the Mall of America, and it's spread out over five hundred acres of beautiful, rolling land. There are nearly four hundred animal species and close to two thousand animals within the Minnesota Zoo, so your grandchild and you will have plenty to see.

Begin your adventure on the Northern Trail, dedicated to mammals. You'll trek along a walkway through prairies and woodlands. Tigers, zebras and bison are just some of the animals you'll encounter (though at times they can be difficult to spot). Off the Northern Trail, wander to the Family Farm, which features a petting zoo that a young grandchild will adore.

Inside the main building is the Tropics Trail—your journey through a rain forest, complete with waterfalls, trees and flowers. Some of the highlights here include the tree kangaroo, the two-toed sloth and the Burmese python.

At the end of the trail, don't miss the wonderful display of fish and other aquatic animals. Here you can actually touch sharks and other sea creatures in an interactive estuary and tide pool. What a thrill!

The Minnesota trail features many animals commonly found in North America. Your grandchild will be more familiar with these species, such as porcupines skunks and snakes.

Other amenities worth noting include a wonderful IMAX theater and a monorail ride providing a narrated overview of the Northern Trail exhibits. Plus the bird and dolphin shows are not to be missed!

Twenty-five years ago, my kids came to the zoo and wandered while I worked. Today, I get to wander with our grandson Matthew and enjoy the exhibits all over again—but this time through new eyes.

Bonding and bridging:

There is an excitement unique to zoos that is shared by young and old alike. We're fascinated by animals, especially those we rarely see. We can watch them from a safe distance and marvel at their grace and beauty.

The zoo also gives us a chance to talk about nature. Why are some animals endangered? What can we do to help them survive? Kids empathize with animals; they want to be good caretakers. We grandparents should nurture that empathy. Use this time to foster in the children a love of animals and a concern for the environment. By doing so, we may help save some endangered species for future generations to enjoy.

A word to the wise:

For a very special treat, there is a program called Dolphin Encounter. If you have a grandchild who is really in love with dolphins, this is the thrill of a lifetime. The three-hour adventure comes with a price tag well over $100, but it includes reserved seats for the dolphin show, a behind-the-scenes tour and a chance to go poolside for a close encounter with one of the dolphins. But that's not all. Your grandchild will also receive a commemorative picture of the experience, as well as a packet of marine conservation information. Some restrictions apply, so contact the Minnesota Zoo for more details.

Age of grandchild: All

Best season: Spring (when the baby animals are born)

Contact: Minnesota Zoo, 13000 Zoo Boulevard, Apple Valley, MN 55124
(800) 366-7811 • info@mnzoo.org • www.mnzoo.org

Also check out:

Como Park Zoo and Conservatory, St. Paul; (651) 487-8200; www.comozooconservatory.org

Lake Superior Zoo, Duluth; (218) 730-4900; www.lszoo.org

Historic Murphy's Landing

Most historical sites concentrate on one location, building, event or era. That's not the case with Historic Murphy's Landing. This unusual attraction is an entire community—with streets, stores, churches and homes. The big difference is that this town happens to span several decades of the 1800s.

You'll find this quiet settlement along the corridor of activity between Highway 169 and the Minnesota River, near Canterbury Downs and Valleyfair. There are forty buildings at Murphy's Landing, covering fifty years of history. They begin with fur trappers and Indian traders and evolve into dreams of a city, prosperity and growth.

This historical venue is filled with variety: the doctor's quarters, a school and a farmhouse, to name a few. Murphy's Landing is a composite of early Minnesota, with wagon rides to shuttle you around and costumed characters to guide you.

Inside the houses, you and your grandchild will gain a sense of what life was like during that particular era. The guides allow you to walk in and truly experience the buildings.

In the summer months, you'll find interpreters (in costume) throughout the village. During the fall, tour guides lead you through the area, and there are special events like a full moon hayride and an antique show, for which you can bring your own artifacts to be appraised.

Walk slowly, take your time, ring the school bell, sit in the shade, and talk to your grandchild about way back when. Can she even imagine what life was like two hundred years ago? Despite the gap in time, it is easy to relate to the settings at Murphy's Landing. You don't have to be a Voyageur, American Indian or soldier. This is a town of "ordinary" people. Here, you could've had a family, worked, gotten involved with the community and spent time visiting neighbors.

At Murphy's Landing, history isn't about famous people and important events. It's everyday people living their everyday lives. That's something important for your grandchild to see.

Bonding and bridging:

At Murphy's Landing, more than anywhere else, your grandchild can see progress take shape. It's like strolling through history, watching how far we advanced in just fifty years during the 1800s. Compare that to where we are today—my what a difference!

Of course, we wouldn't have seen these technological breakthroughs if humans were content by nature. Instead, we are dreamers, imaginers and inventors. Encourage your grandchild to always strive for new answers. Just like Henry Ford and his Model T, if your grandchild keeps searching for better solutions, she has the potential to change the world.

A word to the wise:

Celebrate the Christmas season at Murphy's Landing. On Sundays in December, horse-drawn trolleys carry visitors along snowy lanes, and candles beckon from frosty windows. Each weekend your grandchild and you can be a part of several different holiday settings, enjoy folk artist performances and make traditional crafts that reflect the lifestyles of the river valley settlers.

Age of grandchild: 5 and up

Best season: All

Contact: Historic Murphy's Landing, 2187 East Highway 101, Shakopee, MN 55379 • (763) 694-7784
hmlstaff@ThreeRiversParkDistrict.org
www.threeriversparkdistrict.org/outdoor_ed/murphys_landing

Also check out:

Forest History Center, Grand Rapids; (218) 327-4482; www.mnhs.org/places/sites/fhc/

Freeborn County Museum & Historical Village, Albert Lea; (507) 373-8003; www.smig.net/fchm/historicalvillage.htm

Gibbs Museum, St.Paul; (651) 646-8629; www.rchs.com

Oliver H. Kelley Farm, Elk River; (763) 441-6896; www.mnhs.org/places/sites/ohkf

Minnesota
Landscape Arboretum

Minnesota's four seasons are all dramatically different, and that helps us to appreciate our plants even more. As beautiful as winter's fields of white snow can be, we long for the spring's green. Perhaps that is why so many of us are gardeners and why we can't wait to walk into the Minnesota Landscape Arboretum.

The Arboretum is where your grandchild can run through the grass, sniff the flowers and chase the butterflies. He can listen to the birds' songs, lie on the grass or sit at a picnic table. Together, you can enjoy the Arboretum's many diverse experiences and sensations.

Just some of the areas that are yours to explore include a prairie, a woodland flower area, a Japanese garden and water gardens. Your grandchild will also want to see the bulb gardens, fruit trees and hedges. It's almost a nature over-load—but in a good way.

Hike the trails together. Most of them are easy walks, while some include more challenging landscapes over hills and through woods.

During spring, there is nothing better than a walk supplemented by the fresh smell of crab apples—not to mention flowers in the woodlands and maple syrup sap flowing from the trees. If you're there when the syrup gets made, the scent of that steam will have you dreaming about pancakes for a week.

Summer at the Arboretum is lush, and the prairies are filled with flowers and butterflies. The scent of mowed grass is everywhere, and the herb garden is both pungent and exotic. Next to the main building, you and your grandchild will notice a garden with some extra-special excitement: the buzz and motion of hummingbirds.

In the fall, walk among the crisp leaves, crackling with each step. There is a rich scent of earth and the great beauty of autumn leaves.

It doesn't matter when you visit the Minnesota Landscape Arboretum. You'll find plenty of opportunities for relaxation and enjoyment, and your grand-child will have more than enough space to run around and have fun.

Bonding and bridging:

A tree is the perfect model for your relationship with your grandchild. It must have strong, deep roots in order to grow. It's up to you to provide your grandchild with roots of his own. The time you share together and the lessons you teach are the best ways to help your grandchild develop his roots. The stronger his roots, the more he will grow as a person.

Plant a tree with your grandchild. It can be at your home or his, as long as it's yours to share. Tend to it together, and as your tree grows so too will your grandchild—into an adult of whom you can be proud.

A word to the wise:

The hummingbird garden brings birds and flowers together. The garden's lively combination of colors, scents and sounds is truly a sensory experience. Your grandchild will be thrilled as the hummingbirds buzz around, making the flowers look as if they have come to life.

Age of grandchild: 5 and up

Best season: Spring and fall

Contact: Minnesota Landscape Arboretum, 3675 Arboretum Boulevard, Chaska, MN 55318 • (952) 443-1400 • www.arboretum.umn.edu

Also check out:

Eloise Butler Wildflower Garden, Minneapolis; (612) 370-4903; www.minneapolisparks.org

Leif Erickson Rose Garden, Duluth; (800) 438-5884 (Duluth Convention and Visitors Bureau); www.visitduluth.com

Linnaeus Arboretum (Gustavus Adolphus College), St. Peter; (507) 933-6181; www.gustavus.edu/arboretum

Munsinger Gardens, St. Cloud; (320) 255-7216 (Parks Department); www.munsingerclemens.com

Northland Arboretum, Brainerd; (218) 829-8770; http://arb.brainerd.com

Whatever you love is beautiful; love comes first, beauty follows. The greater your capacity for love, the more beauty you find in the world. JANE SMILEY

Sponsel's Minnesota Harvest

A visit to a farm can be a fun, informative trip for anyone. But Sponsel's Minnesota Harvest takes it one step further. Located in the hills south of Jordan, Sponsel's is a combination of farm and amusement park! With a corn maze on the valley floor and orchards on the slopes, this is the place for good food and good fun.

Apples are Sponsel's mainstay, with numerous varieties on the trees and in the store. In early fall, as you drive your way up the hill toward the entrance, you'll pass through a gauntlet of apple trees and maple sugarbush. The apple trees are bent under the weight of their apples, glimmering in shades of red and green. Each branch is like garland. This beautiful sight is the perfect welcome.

When you arrive at the top of the hill, it is all hustle and bustle. Your grandchild will be in paradise! Take advantage of the courtyard of food, and pick up a few healthy snacks. Then find a nice, shaded spot, and enjoy a picnic in the designated area. A barbecue shack is open for some events, too.

Next, delight your grandchild with a horse or pony ride. You can also share a hayride and a stroll through a mini-maze among the apples. Along the way, your grandkid will be awestruck by the giant pages from the children's book *A is for Apple* (another product of the orchard).

No visit is complete without a look inside the store. For background music, a player piano operates continuously. You can sit and relax or shop for freshly baked goods and farm products such as honey, syrup, cider and apples. You and your grandchild can sample the varieties and choose your favorites— though with all of the names and descriptions available, it is hard to decide on the best.

A trip to Sponsel's Minnesota Harvest is about much more than an afternoon of fun. It's a celebration of health, and it sets an example for choosing a healthy lifestyle and for eating good foods. Who knows? Maybe next time you go to the store, your grandchild will ask for an apple instead of a candy bar.

Bonding and bridging:

When you think about a maze, you probably think of a fun, challenging activity. But there are a lot of lessons to be learned from being inside one. How our grandchildren approach a maze is the same way that they should approach all of life's obstacles.

Often, your grandchild won't be quite sure if she's following the correct path, and more often than not she'll hit a roadblock or dead end. If she gets frustrated and stops trying, she's finished. But if she remains calm and keeps a positive attitude, she can work her way backward and begin again. With patience, hard work and perhaps a little help from her grandparent, she'll be through that maze in no time!

A word to the wise:

If you remember picking corn and running through corn rows as a child, then the corn maze is a great way to introduce your grandkid to a piece of your childhood. Watch with delight as she gets excited about the mystery and challenge that unfolds. It is a new landscape, one that is both a setting and a game. Try it, then take some corn home and cook it up!

Age of grandchild: 8 and up

Best season: Fall

Contact: Sponsel's Minnesota Harvest, Old Highway 169 Boulevard at Apple Lovers' Lane, Jordan, MN 55352 • (800) 662-7753 minnesotaharvest@aol.com • www.minnesotaharvest.net

Also check out:

For a listing of all orchards, visit www.applejournal.com

Some family trees bear an enormous crop of nuts. WAYNE H.

National
Eagle Center

There's a reason why the eagle was chosen as our nation's symbol, and the first time I saw one I understood why: These amazing animals are awe-inspiring and powerful. As fascinating as eagles are to grandparents, they are ten times more interesting to children, making the National Eagle Center a must-visit.

You'll find the center in Wabasha, on the banks of the Mississippi River. The town offers an ideal location because it is a gathering place for wintering bald eagles. In fact eagles adorn the trees like Christmas decorations, and they

fish the ice-lined waters from Reads Landing through this expanse of the Upper Mississippi River Wildlife and Fish Refuge. Seeing all of the eagles is one of the most impressive winter sights in Minnesota and well worth a visit in January or February.

Plans to build a larger, more elaborate center are underway, but the beginning of the National Eagle Center is rooted in a storefront operation on Main Street Wabasha. For now, the center is small and intimate, which is perfect because it allows you to see the eagles up close. You and your grandchild will also find books and eagle memorabilia, a table for coloring, videos, displays and the intangible but intense energy that the staff emits.

This visit will get your grandchild closer to our national emblem than any zoo can. He'll marvel at the bird's size, beak, talons and sounds. The six-foot wingspan, majestic patterns and an air of independence—even while sitting on a perch in the corner—make this bird something very special to see.

Throughout the rest of the year, from March to December, many eagles still call the Wabasha area home. Up to thirty nesting pairs remain in the region, and they can be observed from a variety of locations along the river highway.

If you hope to develop in your grandchild a love of animals, a trip to the National Eagle Center is a wonderful starting point. The Mississippi River and its eagles make a great combination for experiencing nature, and the National Eagle Center is the place to celebrate these magnificent creatures.

Bonding and bridging:

The story of how we almost lost the Bald Eagle is as full of meaning and drama as any story we can tell. Imagine these magnificent birds disappearing. Chemicals were killing them (and were silently killing us too). Thanks to the courageous work of Rachel Carson, action was taken to save this endangered species. The chemicals were reduced, and the eagle population rose.

If your grandchild ever asks, "What can I do? How can one person make a difference? How can I save the world all by myself?" You need only tell him the story of Rachel Carson, the woman who saved the Bald Eagle. If she could do that, there's no telling what your grandchild might accomplish.

A word to the wise:

There is no bad time to visit the National Eagle Center, but January through March is by far the best. During cold and snowy winters, adult eagles will congregate along the shore, in leafless trees and along the tributaries. It is exciting to see these large, white-headed birds as they hunt and rest. For some extra fun, travel along this stretch of river and do a census. Count the birds you see. Make it a challenge. Find your way to Winona and join all of the volunteers on the observation platforms. These wonderful guides will help you see the birds and will even share their scopes!

Age of grandchild: All

Best season: Winter

Contact: National Eagle Center, 152 West Main,
Wabasha, MN 55981 • (877) 332-4537
info@nationaleaglecenter.org • www.nationaleaglecenter.org

Also check out:

Gabbert Raptor Center (University of Minnesota), St. Paul; (612) 624-4745; www.raptor.cvm.umn.edu

Vince Shute Wildlife Sanctuary, Orr; (218) 757-0172; www.americanbear.org

Wildlife Science Center, Forest Lake; (651) 464-3993; www.wildlifesciencecenter.org

All things are connected, like the blood which connects one family. Whatever befalls the earth befalls the children of the earth. CHIEF SEATTLE

L.A.R.K.
Toy Store

L.A.R.K. Toy Store should come with a warning: Be prepared for overload—an imagination overload! Your grandchild won't be the only one who is overwhelmed. L.A.R.K. Toy Store is the place for people of all ages to let go of their inhibitions, where play is king, where design and art meld, where shopping and games come together.

Who would imagine such a place exists just outside the quiet river town of Kellogg south of Wabasha? This grandchild's paradise has it all: an outdoor miniature golf course, an indoor carousel, a bookstore, a candy store, a wood-craft workshop and—oh, yes—a toy store!

The store is an outgrowth of the creative efforts of Donn and Sarah Kreofsky. For fun they started making wooden toys. Other people took notice, and the orders started piling up. The rest, as they say, is history.

L.A.R.K. Toy Store is an indoor mall that resembles a wooden lodge. With so much to choose from, it's hard to say what the main attraction is. However, it just might be the amazing carousel. Your grandchild can choose to ride any of the carousel's twenty hand-carved, wooden creatures including dragons and otters. It's quite a sight to behold!

Another favorite spot is the Troll Toy Shop. Who wouldn't want to have a toy dinosaur, a hopping rabbit or a rocking dragon? There's also Boomer Heaven with its antique toys that you'll remember from your childhood, the Museum Shop that showcases rare collectibles and the Christmas Shop for unusual holiday decorations including L.A.R.K.'s own miniature village.

Stop into the Plane Bakery for delicious baked goods, as well as a chance to glimpse model airplanes flying overhead. And finally head into the bookstore where you can choose from the two thousand titles in stock.

L.A.R.K., which stands for "Lost Arts Revival by Kreofsky," has been open since 1983. All of the items sold are either handmade or handpicked by the owners, so you know you're getting a quality item with every purchase. The trick with a visit to L.A.R.K. Toy Store isn't having fun; it's stopping yourself from buying everything in sight!

Bonding and bridging:

Remember all of those cool toys we used to play with? We didn't have video games or computers. Our toys didn't talk, transform or move on their own. But we still had plenty of fun. Kids' toys nowadays are quite different.

L.A.R.K. Toy Store is a chance for you to show your grandchild how toys used to be. She will be amazed by the simple toys and their many colors and designs. Share your experiences of playing with these old-fashioned toys. You just might spark a new interest within your grandchild, and getting kids away from their video games—even for a little while—makes for much healthier imaginations.

A word to the wise:

The carousel is a rotating work of art that cannot be described. Its creatures are wooden, finely detailed sculptures of plants and animals not commonly found on merry-go-rounds. Many sculptures feature complete ecosystems. This carousel is a lesson in biology presented in a way that makes it fun for children to find the details.

Age of grandchild: 16 months to 13 years

Best season: All

Contact: L.A.R.K. Toy Store, PO Box 39, Lark Lane, Kellogg, MN 55945 (507) 767-3387 • lark@wabasha.net • www.larktoys.com

Also check out:

Creative Kids Stuff, Minneapolis; (800) 353-0710; www.creativekidstuff.com

Legoland (Mall of America), Bloomington; (952) 858-8949; www.lego.com

Wonderment, Linden Hills; (612) 929-2707; www.wondermentshop.com

I like to do nice things for my grandchildren—like buy them those toys I've always wanted to play with. Gene Perret

Root River
State Trail

Minnesota is full of beautiful trails and locations, but the Root River State Trail is perhaps the best of them all. The scenery is incomparable, thanks in large part to the ancient geological forces that created the southeast's unique hills and valleys. The soil is a rich, dark, alluvial sediment, creating some of the best farmland in the valleys. And the steep bluffs are thick with forests.

The Root River Trail is as close as we get to mountains in Minnesota. As the name implies, the trail closely follows the path of the Root River, beginning in the town of Houston—a perfect place for a bicycle ride with a grandchild. Before departing, take a look around the nature center, which serves as the trail's starting point. You'll both enjoy the whimsical, recycled-bike-part sculptures in front of the center.

The trail winds forty-two miles to its western terminus at the town of Fountain. Because the trail is in the valley, it is mostly flat and easy for all ages, but there is one half-mile stretch of steep hills between Houston and Rushford, which may not be suitable for all bikers.

Decide beforehand how far you wish to go. Choose a comfortable distance for you and your grandchild. This should be a pleasant sightseeing experience. Of course, forty-two miles is probably too far, but the trail does pass through the quaint villages of Whalen and Peterson, as well as the charming towns of Lanesboro and Rushford. Brick storefronts and Victorian houses abound!

The longest distance between two towns is 12.6 miles from Houston to Rushford. The closest together are Lanesboro and Whalen at 4.6 miles. Parking for the trail is found in all of the towns, and there are numerous picnic areas and campgrounds along the way, plus a lot of places to eat, sleep, shop and rent bicycles.

Further supplementing your journey, you'll find forty-seven redecked railroad bridges. As you cross over the river, you may see canoeists or tubers going by. The Root River has a steady current most of the year, so it is a popular choice for these types of activities.

For an outdoor Minnesota experience, biking the Root River Trail is a must.

Bonding and bridging:

You may never be able to travel to Switzerland and the Alps with your grandchild, but as you bicycle through the towering hills of the Root River Trail, you might as well be there! Biking, much like walking, encourages observation and conversation, and it's good for your grandchild to see his grandparent participating and enjoying an aerobic activity such as biking. Sure, it's a fun recreation, but it also sets a good example for a lifetime of health and activity. Plus it lets your grandchild know that we don't always need a combustion engine to get places and to have fun.

A word to the wise:

There is nothing like the deciduous forest for wildflowers, and the Houston Nature Center has wonderful hiking trails to observe them. These woods are a vivid palette of colors and shapes, especially in April and May when flowers bloom as the sun warms the earth. It is a brief period of time and one of the best times to bicycle.

Age of grandchild: 7 and up

Best season: Spring, summer and fall

Contact: Rochester Area Trails & Waterways (Douglas, Root River and Harmony-Preston Valley Trails), 2300 Silver Creek Road Northeast, Rochester, MN 55906 • (507) 285-7176

Also check out:

Minnesota DNR (state trails); (888) 646-6367; www.dnr.state.mn.us/state_trails

Minnesota Trails; www.mntrails.com

Parks & Trails Council of Minnesota; (800) 944-0707; www.parksandtrails.org

Trails from Rails; www.trailsfromrails.com

Mystery Cave

In most people's minds a cave conjures up images of a dark, dripping, cold abyss, filled with lurking dangers and bats. Caves are, in fact, dark. And many do harbor hibernating bats, but these winged mammals do not generally fly around waiting to get caught in your hair. In truth, they would prefer to remain as far away from you as you would from them. Mystery Cave in south-eastern Minnesota is a great place to introduce grandchildren to these dark caverns—while debunking the myths that caves are homes to monsters and other hidden evils.

With more than thirteen miles of natural passages, Mystery Cave is the longest in Minnesota. It was incorporated into Forestville State Park in 1988.

A new and beautiful visitor center opened in 2004. Inside, you can buy your tour tickets, and you will find several excellent exhibits describing the cave and its history. Of course, there is also a gift shop where you can buy your grandchild a souvenir.

The cave's trails are ramped, concrete walkways, which make it one of the few wheelchair-accessible caves in the country. Recessed lights make walking the half-mile route safe and less intimidating for everyone. On the walk, you and your grandchild will encounter flowstone, fins, stalactites, fossils and a beautiful turquoise pool. You may also get to see the blind, colorless springtail insects.

On summer weekends, a special two-hour tour is available in the afternoon. During this tour, you will travel nearly a mile down the gravel paths (including several steps up and down) and into larger passages with fewer formations. Plan on wearing a jacket or sweater on either tour, because the damp, chilled air will soon have you shivering.

Oh, yes, and you may see a few bats too. Approximately three thousand little brown bats call Mystery Cave home during early spring and late fall. You might find it a little creepy, but most grandkids will think it's cool.

Bonding and bridging:

There's something exciting and mysterious about exploring a cave. It's foreign and unknown, and a child almost feels as if he's discovering uncharted territory—a place where no one else has ever been.

As grandparents, we may feel the thrill ourselves when we enter Mystery Cave, though it won't be as strong as our grandchildren's. It's up to us to cultivate their yearning to explore the unknown. As we build in them an enthusiasm for discovery, we are leading them toward a bright future, filled with knowledge and insight.

A word to the wise:

If you're feeling up to it and if your grandchild is at least thirteen years old, you'll share quite an experience by going on a real caving (spelunking) tour. Each four-hour adventure teaches you true caving techniques with a lot of crawling and squeezing through small spaces. This amazing adventure is not for the unfit or for the claustrophobic, but it's sure to send your "cool" factor off the charts! The caving tours are only offered on Saturdays (and some Sundays) between Memorial Day and Labor Day.

Age of grandchild: 6 and up (young kids should take the one-hour tour)

Best season: Summer

Contact: Forestville/Mystery Cave State Park, Route 2, Box 128, Preston, MN 55965 • (507) 937-3251
www.dnr.state.mn.us/state_parks/forestville_mystery_cave

Also check out:

Jeffers Petroglyphs, Jeffers; (507) 628-5591; www.mnhs.org/places/sites/jp

Niagara Cave, Harmony; (800) 837-6606; www.exploreminnesota.com/Niagara_Cave_in_Harmony_with_Nature.html

Pipestone National Monument, Pipestone; (507) 825-5464; www.nps.gov/pipe

Pipestone
National Monument

It's hard to imagine a more significant Minnesota site for American Indian history than Pipestone National Monument. Located in the southwest corner of Minnesota, Pipestone was a central location for many Indian nations and a unique place of peace. Despite any warfare that might exist elsewhere, this was a spot where all animosity was put aside, where anyone of American Indian ancestry could and still can dig in harmony with all other Indians.

The monument includes a visitor center filled with interesting information and exhibits, as well as a scenic trail to hike. Be sure to bring your grandchild inside first. Show her the Native American Culture Center, which features numerous exhibits about the site's history, including a new petroglyph display. Watch the eight-minute orientation program; it will help prepare you for the tour of the grounds. Finally, before hitting the trail, stop at the front desk and ask for a Junior Ranger Guidebook, which will enhance your walk by giving you and your grandchild some challenges to do.

The circular trail, which is less than a mile long and is wheelchair accessible, meanders along a stream until you reach Winnewissa Falls. This is a good place to stop in the shade of the rocks. Just let the quiet sounds of nature soak in.

As you continue your trek, you'll find several landmarks identified by signs. Your grandchild will have a lot of fun learning about each site's significance, whether it's seeing a face in these red rocks or finding a place where young Indians would come of age by jumping across a frightening abyss.

The active quarries along the trail are off limits, but if someone is working when you walk by, you are welcome to quietly observe them. Near the end of the trail, you'll see Exhibit Quarry. This is a place where visitors are allowed to walk into an old excavation site to examine the rocks more closely.

Once you arrive back at the center, your grandchild can turn in her completed trail sheet to receive a certificate and Pipestone National Monument Junior Ranger Badge. If she (or you) can't answer all of the questions, a park ranger will help you.

Bonding and bridging:

American Indians were centuries ahead of the rest of the world. The Pipestone Quarry may very well have been our first version of the United Nations. Here natives from every tribe came together in a location of peace. Battles and disputes were forgotten. It was a place without violence and a place without worry.

If only the rest of us had such a spot in today's world. There is hatred and war at every turn. We must teach our grandchildren a better way. Start small, by demonstrating to your grandchild what empathy and compassion mean. If she can develop these characteristics and put them to use with her siblings, her friends and even the kids that get picked on at school, your grandchild will grow into a person who stands for peace.

A word to the wise:

Inside the monument's visitor center, you'll find American Indian crafts-people making pipes. For your grandchild (and for you), this is a way to see an ancient Dakota tradition that's still being practiced; it helps her realize how a place can be significant in different ways to different people. This is also a good opportunity to talk about the places in your family that may have significance for you but not necessarily for others.

Age of grandchild: 8 and up

Best season: Summer

Contact: Pipestone National Monument, 36 Reservation Avenue, Pipestone, MN 56164 • (507) 825-5464 • www.nps.gov/pipe

Also check out:

Grand Portage National Monument, Grand Portage; (218) 475-2202; www.nps.gov/grpo

Jeffers Petroglyphs, Jeffers; (507) 628-5591; www.mnhs.org/places/sites/jp/

Stearns History Museum (quarry), St. Cloud; (866) 253-8424; www.stearns-museum.org

I like to walk with Grandpa, his steps are short like mine.
He doesn't say, "Now hurry up." He always takes his time. UNKNOWN

Walnut Grove

It's a book, it's a TV show, and it's a place in southwest Minnesota. While your grandchild is too young to remember *Little House on the Prairie* (unless he watches it in syndication), a trip to Walnut Grove is a chance to see literature come alive.

The town was made famous through the writings of Laura Ingalls Wilder, who documented her family's 1874 journey to Walnut Grove in a series of children's books. Her family's first home was a one-room sod dugout on the banks of Plum Creek—a place that you and your grandchild can still visit today. All that remains of Laura's childhood home is a deep depression in the ground, but it's amazing to see the plum thickets, table lands, big rock and other landmarks Laura described in her first book *On the Banks of Plum Creek*.

The Laura Ingalls Wilder Museum is another must-see. Actually a collection of interesting buildings, the museum includes an 1898 depot, a chapel, an onion-domed house, a little red schoolhouse, an early settler home and a

covered wagon. Inside, you can browse the exhibits such as Laura's handmade quilt, memorabilia from the television show and fascinating artifacts from early Walnut Grove. There's a quaint little gift shop too, where you can purchase books, bonnets, hand-crafted items and other souvenirs.

The event of the summer in Walnut Grove is its annual Wilder Pageant. Held every July in a wonderful hillside amphitheater, the pageant tells the tale of Laura and her family, from their arrival in Walnut Grove through tragedies such as prairie fires and Mary's blindness and all the way to their decision to leave Walnut Grove. The live performance is an excellent picture of Minnesota life in the 1870s.

Another annual tradition is the Laura-Nellie Look-Alike contest. Girls, ages eight to twelve, can dress up like either Laura or Nellie and enter. Win or lose, this event is fun for everyone!

A sense of Minnesota history, an entertaining atmosphere and an excuse to get your grandchild excited about reading—Walnut Grove is the perfect place for a grandparent-grandchild visit.

Bonding and bridging:

Little House on the Prairie is one of the best family shows that has ever been on television. It's a model of a loving family, it's filled with lessons about honesty and integrity, and every episode has a happy ending. However, historical accuracy is not among the show's strengths.

If your grandchild is more familiar with the TV show than he is with the books, he may be quite shocked when he discovers what life was really like for the Ingalls. Their home wasn't large and spacious, there are no mountains near Walnut Grove, and the Ingalls weren't successful there. In fact, they left after just a few years. This is a great chance for you to point out that not everything your grandchild sees and hears on the TV is true. Television's main function is to entertain—not to inform. A much better source for a grandchild who's eager to learn is his local library. If you can, choose a night every week to turn off the television, and take him to the library instead.

A word to the wise:

Before your visit, read *On the Banks of Plum Creek* with your grandchild, and watch a few episodes of *Little House on the Prairie* together (in syndication or available on DVD). You'll be amazed at how many times you can say, "Do you remember that from the book," and "That's not how it was on the TV show." What a wonderful learning experience—for both of you!

Age of grandchild: 7 and up

Best season: Summer

Contact: Laura Ingalls Wilder Museum, 330 Eighth Street, Walnut Grove, MN 56180 • (800) 528-7280 • www.walnutgrove.org

Also check out:

Judy Garland Museum, Grand Rapids; (800) 664-5839; www.judygarlandmuseum.com

Song of Hiawatha Pageant, Pipestone; (800) 430-4126; www.pipestoneminnesota.com/pageant

Historic Chippewa City

There's something fascinating about comparing lifestyles of a hundred years ago to lifestyles of today. Grandchildren long to discover how things were done "way back when" and are amazed to learn how far we've come since that time. Few places give us as in-depth a look as Historic Chippewa City in Montevideo.

A project that began in 1965, Chippewa City now encompasses twenty-three historic buildings. It is a diverse collection of structures that captures the essence of life between the mid 1800s and the early 1900s.

Your journey into Chippewa City starts as you and your grandchild pass through the Gateway Building. Inside you'll find the Anderson Interpretive Center, the library, a resource center and a gift shop.

As you exit the building, your first stops are the Millinery and Dress Shop and the old Print Shop. If your grandchild is familiar with computers, she's sure to get a kick out of the old linotype, typewriters and presses. She'll have a hard time believing that newspapers and other documents were ever printed this way.

Next, swing through the Law Office on your way to the Fire Department—a very popular spot that features a 1914 Fire Engine. Browns Brother Fuel and Ice is also worth noting. It Illustrates how people got their ice before the age of refrigerators. Connected to Browns Brother is the Buggy Shop, which houses an 1880 horse drawn hearse, a buggy, a cutter and a surrey. Those relics are certainly fun to see!

There's plenty more too; in fact, you're not even halfway yet. A post office, a bank and a blacksmith shop all give glimpses into the working life of your grandchild's ancestors. Plus, the old schoolhouse will have special relevance for her. Furnishings inside include desks, a bench, lamps and maps—as well as the school's original wood shed and outhouses just outside.

There are many excellent places in Minnesota that show us pieces of the past, but none rival Historic Chippewa City as an attraction that demonstrates the structural foundation of an old city: its businesses, schools and churches.

Bonding and bridging:

Every town in Minnesota has a unique story. Many were formed near waterways, and some were born from the railroad. As soon as enough people came together, their needs had to be met. Schools were built, stores were raised, and post offices brought the mail.

Take your grandchild on a tour of her hometown. Show her a few schools and churches. Bring her to the police station, the court house and the post office. A bank and a grocery store are also excellent stops. Go inside whenever you can. The more you show her, the more curious she'll become. Explain to her what each of these places is for and why a town needs it. This valuable lesson will serve to raise your grandchild's awareness of her town and will also take her one step closer to understanding how the world works.

A word to the wise:

Grandchildren love fire trucks. That's why the Historic Chippewa City Fire Department is always a favorite stop. Your grandchild is welcome to ring the fire bell outside the building, and the fully restored 1914 Seagraves Fire Engine is sure to make an impression. Plus, it still runs and can be seen in parades from time to time. If you can, plan ahead so your grandchild can see the Fire Engine in action at a local parade (such as the Grand Day Parade on Father's Day).

Age of grandchild: 5 and up

Best season: Summer

Contact: Chippewa County Historical Society,
Junction Highway 7 and Highway 59, Montevideo, MN 56265
(320) 269-7636 • cchs.june@juno.com
www.montechamber.com/cchs/cchshp.htm

Also check out:

Freeborn County Museum & Historical Village, Albert Lea; (507) 373-8003; www.smig.net/fchm/historicalvillage.htm

Nobles County Pioneer Village, Worthington; (507) 376-4431; www.noblespioneervillage.com

Sinclair Lewis Days

No other state houses the birthplace of America's first winner of the Nobel Prize in Literature, but Minnesota does. Sinclair Lewis was born in Sauk Centre in 1885, and the town proudly celebrates its legendary author every year during Sinclair Lewis Days.

Lewis, who wrote *Main Street*, *Babbitt* and *Arrowsmith*, was considered the conscience of his generation. He was ahead of his time, writing about issues involving women, race and the poor. Much of what he wrote in the 1920s still holds true today. This is certainly a man worthy of honoring.

Sauk Centre's weeklong festival features everything you would expect in a community celebration—and more. The event kicks off with a treasure hunt for $100, and as you approach midweek, the town livens up with basketball tournaments, turtle races, a kiddie parade and a concert in the park.

On Thursday night, Miss Sauk Centre is crowned. Then, when the weekend arrives, you and your grandchild can enjoy everything from a craft show and flea market to sports tournaments and the Sinclair Lewis Days Parade. Finally, on Sunday, relax and enjoy music in the park and a fireworks display at dusk.

While you are in town for the festival, make time to stop at the Sinclair Lewis Interpretive Center and his boyhood home. Inside the center, you and your grandchild can view several interesting artifacts such old photographs, Lewis's writing desk, various personal items and his Nobel prize. His boyhood home offers a glimpse of the life that Lewis referenced so frequently in his books. The furniture, cookstove and desk are all reminiscent of a not-so-distant time.

Some people deserve to be celebrated, and Sinclair Lewis is one such person. Introduce your grandchild to a man who made a difference, whose writings are relevant to so many people spanning generation after generation. Perhaps this visit will spark your grandchild to write the next "Great American Novel."

Bonding and bridging:

Writing is one of those skills that everyone uses. At work and at home, it's a part of our everyday lives—whether we're creating a resume, sending our family and friends an email, or penning a book. It's unlikely that your grandchild will become "the next Sinclair Lewis" (although anything is possible), but writing is a talent that we should help him develop.

Spend time with your grandchild dedicated to reading and to writing. When you're at home, read together instead of watching television. When you're out exploring Minnesota, bring along a journal. Help your grandchild write about what he sees and feels, about what he likes and doesn't like about each trip. Soon, writing may become a habit for him, and with the right encouragement from you, he may even grow to love it. The ability to write well is key to his future. With it, he is far more likely to succeed, regardless of the field he chooses.

A word to the wise:

Among the most interesting displays inside the Sinclair Lewis Interpretive Center is "Birth of a Novel." It details the techniques that Lewis used to name his characters and to create their fictitious biographies, as well as a map and description of a fictional city. This peek into the mind of a brilliant writer is very interesting to see, and it may even inspire your grandchild to create a world of characters all his own.

Age of grandchild: All

Best season: Summer

Contact: Sauk Centre Chamber of Commerce, Junction I-94 and Highway 71, Sauk Centre, MN 56378 • (320) 352-5201
chamber@saukcentrechamber.com • www.saukcentrechamber.com

Also check out:

Father Hennepin Festival, Champlin; (763) 923-7193; http://ci.champlin.mn.us

Judy Garland Festival, Grand Rapids; (800) 664-5839; www.judygarlandmuseum.com

Itasca State Park

Minnesota's first state park is perhaps the best and is certainly the most historic. Itasca State Park is where you'll find the source of the Mississippi River, but it represents so much more.

This place is also the finish line of a legendary search to discover where the mighty Mississippi began. With names like Nicollet, Long, Pike, Carver and Schoolcraft, the headwaters boasts a "who's who" list of mid-continent explorers.

The legendary river winds a curving, circuitous route from Lake Itasca, now recognized as the headwaters, to the Gulf of Mexico. It may be a gargantuan river with a vital and storied past, but its beginnings are quite humble to say the least.

At the Itasca headwaters, you can walk across this great river in just a few strides. It's hard to imagine that this tiny stream becomes a roaring river that dissects the entire country.

Of course, if Itasca State Park were just about the headwaters, it wouldn't be quite as wonderful. There is plenty of other wilderness to enjoy.

For instance, you'll find some of the most beautiful growths of old pines in the country. You and your grandchild will marvel at the incredible, lake-studded forests.

Particularly with grandchildren who are a little older, you'll want to spend some time exploring. Hike the trails or bring a couple of bikes. Perhaps you even want to do some boating around the lakes. For your convenience, you'll find a set of lodges and a visitors' center filled with helpful information.

If you hope to foster in your grandchild a deep love of nature, a trip to Itasca State Park should be at the top of your "to do" list. Neither one of you will regret the experience.

Bonding and bridging:

Who would've guessed that the country's mighty Mississippi River begins as nothing more than a stream? That's what makes Itasca State Park's headwaters such a special place for grandchildren. Here, dreaming is born. If this tiny trickle of water can become our nation's greatest river, anything is possible. Boys can grow up to be artists. Girls can become astronauts. All it takes is a dream and a desire to do something about it. As the Mississippi River demonstrates, once we begin something, the sky's the limit as to how far we can go!

A word to the wise:

I have stood at the source of the Mississippi and watched for hours as adults and children found their ways across the rocky beginning of the river. Laughter, wet feet and an accidental slip every once in a while are all part of the experience. You are touching water that will eventually be in the Gulf of Mexico; your presence will pass secretly through locks and dams, past sleepy towns and large cities. It is a 2,552-mile journey of wild imagination. This captivating experience amuses everyone who crosses.

Age of grandchild: 5 and up

Best season: Summer and fall

Contact: Itasca State Park, 36750 Main Park Drive,
Park Rapids, MN 56470 • (218) 266-2100 • itasca.park@dnr.state.mn.us.
www.dnr.state.mn.us/state_parks/itasca

Also check out:

Big Stone Lake State Park (source of the Red River of the North and the Minnesota River), Montevideo; (320) 839-3663; www.dnr.state.mn.us/state_parks/big_stone_lake

Forget not that the earth delights to feel your bare feet, and the winds long to play with your hair. KAHLIL GIBRAN

Forest
History Center

Timber! Daylight in the swamp! It's December 1900 in the logging camp, and there is a lot to be done in these cold, short days if the lumberjacks are going to make any money this season.

It may actually be July and ninety degrees outside, but don't tell that to the costumed actors of the lumberjack days, as you visit the Forest History Center and learn about the peak of logging in Minnesota. Lumbering has been a big part of Minnesota's past and present. The forest was important to American Indians and to everyone who immigrated to this territory. Forests provided raw materials for shelter and were abundant sources of food.

At the Forest History Center, you and your grandchild will see first-hand the important part that lumbering played in the lifestyles and survival of settlers. Let your grandchild follow the center's guide, time travel in her mind and get into the experience. The logging camp is complete with realistic furnishings and characters.

Begin your journey at the Interpretive Building, with films and displays that help set the stage for this historical visit. From there, you and your grandchild can join a guided, one-hour tour or explore on your own. (We prefer the tour.) You will be led through the logging camp, where your grandchild can interact with everyone from cooks to lumberjacks to blacksmiths.

There is also a river wanigan from the summer of 1901, a forest service cabin locked into 1934 and a hundred-foot fire tower from which she can keep watch for forest fires. In case that's not enough, the two of you can also explore the center's three nature trails.

A trip to Minnesota's Forest History Center provides perspectives, questions and challenges. It is a good place to discuss our personal actions, as well as our relationship to the forest. Plan a trip to Grand Rapids, and discover this wonderful attraction for your grandchild and for yourself.

Bonding and bridging:

What is the value of looking at our past? Why do we do it? These are questions that your grandchild is bound to wonder, and there are no simple answers. You can say that we look at where we've been to see how far we've come—to see how much we've progressed. We preserve our history so we can share it with others—so we can share our tragedies, as well as our triumphs.

After your visit to the Forest History Center, encourage your grandchild to begin preserving her own history. Suggest that she start keeping a journal. Perhaps you'll even want to buy her one. Someday, she'll look back fondly at the memories of her childhood, and she will one day cherish the opportunity to share them with grandchildren of her own.

A word to the wise:

To truly experience the enthusiasm and energy of lumberjack times, bring your grandchild to the Forest History Center for one of their special events. A few to choose from include the metalsmith gathering, storytelling and music day, and the day on which they demonstrate real horse power.

Age of grandchild: 5 and up

Best season: Summer (though there are a few winter events too)

Contact: Forest History Center, 2609 County Road 76, Grand Rapids, MN 55744 • (218) 327-4482
foresthistory@mnhs.org • www.mnhs.org/places/sites/fhc/

Also check out:

Chippewa National Forest Visitor Centers, Cass Lake; (218) 335-8600; www.fs.fed.us/r9/forests/chippewa

Cloquet Forestry Center, Cloquet; (218) 726-6400; www.cnr.umn.edu/cfc

Minnesota Landscape Arboretum, Chaska; (952) 443-1400; www.arboretum.umn.edu

Superior National Forest Visitor Centers, Duluth; (218) 626-4300; www.fs.fed.us/r9/forests/superior

To our children we give two things: one is roots, the other wings. ANDY ROONEY

Judy Garland Museum

Quick, name a sixty-five-year-old movie that children around the world still adore today! Need a hint? The leading lady spent her early childhood right here in Minnesota. Of course, we're talking about *The Wizard of Oz* and our own Judy Garland.

Fortunately, the city of Grand Rapids has saved and restored Judy's birthplace and childhood home, giving us the one-of-a-kind Judy Garland Museum. It preserves a lifestyle and family home from the first World War and is valuable for that reason alone. But this tourist attraction goes much further.

A time capsule of the early 1920s, the museum takes us back to June 10, 1922, when Judy Garland—or rather Frances Ethel Gumm—was born. She lived with her family in that very home for four and a half years before moving to California.

Previous to visiting the Judy Garland Museum, be sure to watch the movie with your grandchild. Then it's off to see the wonderful exhibits and displays. You'll get a look into the life and music of Judy, which is quite fascinating for

us older folks. Don't be surprised if the Children's Discovery Museum next door is more of a draw for the grandkids, since they remember Dorothy of Oz and not Judy (or Frances) of Grand Rapids. See first-hand the movie memorabilia, and use it as a starting point for talking and for sharing.

The paper doll and cutout exhibit is fun for everyone, and so are the face cutouts in front and inside. They make excellent opportunities for family photographs.

There is a gift store, and—as mentioned before—the Children's Discovery Museum is filled with rooms that offer kids a chance to move in their own land of Oz. Save ample time for your grandchild to play in this area.

Not many movies cross so many generations and stay fresh and exciting. A 1939 film that is familiar to today's children is a great tool for connecting the generational gap.

Bonding and bridging:

There's no avoiding it. Today's celebrities are our grandchildren's role models. Whether it's right or wrong and whether we like it or not, they grow up idolizing their favorite movie stars and sports heroes. By visiting the Judy Garland Museum, we get a glimpse into the life of someone famous. Your grandchild may be surprised to discover that his home is not that different from theirs (aside from its 1920s setup).

Use this chance to ask questions about why your grandchild idolizes celebrities. What makes them so special? Does your grandchild really know what kind of people those celebrities are? There are real heroes all around your grandchild: his teachers, his parents, local firemen and police officers—and, of course, his grandparents. Perhaps now is the time for your grandchild to take notice of the people who truly make a difference in his life.

A word to the wise:

Each June since 1975 Grand Rapids has hosted the Judy Garland Festival. A few of the original Munchkins continue to visit the annual event. In addition, Dorothy and the other characters come alive in costume to make the festival a truly wizardly experience. Your grandchild and you will get plenty of thrills from the guest celebrities, seminars, talent shows, films and other events to fill up the weekend!

Age of grandchild: 6 to 13

Best season: Summer

Contact: Judy Garland Museum, 2727 Highway 169 South,
PO Box 724, Grand Rapids, MN 55744 • (800) 664-5839
jgarland@uslink.net • www.judygarlandmuseum.com

Also check out:

Laura Ingalls Wilder Museum, Walnut Grove; (800) 528-7280; www.walnutgrove.org

Acting is just a way of making a living; the family is life. Denzel Washington

Ironworld

In a thin line across northeastern Minnesota, you'll find the Iron Range, one of the most unique and historic landscapes in the state. This is where the majority of iron was mined to support both World Wars. The story of the Iron Range is so big that it's hard to grasp. Thankfully, we have the help of a place called Ironworld.

Ironworld is a museum—and then some! It tells the geologic story of the region, the creation of the minerals and the landscape, and about the Iron Rangers, a group of people who came to extract raw ore. The story of their lives is something you can help your grandchild understand. Can she imagine having to move into a new house because it's time to remove the ore under her parents' land?

Outside the museum, the two of you can explore a variety of interpretive sites with actors playing the roles of weavers, cooks, wood carvers and gardeners.

They'll engage you to discuss what life was like outside the mines. To add to the experience, you and your grandchild can climb aboard one of the 1928 Melbourne Trolleys. Every child loves a train ride, and the Mesabi Railroad Trolley route is short but scenic. It will take you past great vistas and into the village of Glen.

Before 1935, there were more than fifty homes in this mining village, and the actors bring those homes back to life. Explore as if you were visiting your relatives. If you're lucky, you may even be treated to freshly baked cookies. At last, the time must come to hop back on the trolley and begin your trip home.

The Iron Range has always had its own personality. Because it was isolated from the rest of the state and the people who lived here came directly from their European lands, the independent miners were called Rangers. Our grandchildren do not know the Iron Range as we do. This is a story that can be fun to tell, but keep in mind that you are their gateway to discovering this unique place.

Bonding and bridging:

Can you ever imagine leaving your family behind, heading to unknown territory, working long days with no hope of seeing any loved ones? This was the life of the Iron Ranger, and they chose it out of love. These brave men sacrificed happiness and comfort so their families would not go without.

The sacrifices your grandchild witnesses may not be as apparent. However, those who love her make sacrifices every day. Ironworld offers a chance to help your grandchild realize how much she is loved and how grateful she should be for those who take care of her. Ask her if she can think of any sacrifices that her parents have made, and help her to realize just how much she depends on her loved ones.

A word to the wise:

There is a lot to take in at Ironworld, but the best part is most definitely the trolley ride and visit to the town of Glen. Your grandchild and you can ride it into a world that is unlike any other place in Minnesota. You'll both see a magnificent view of the pits—now lakes—ringed with green trees beneath walls of red. Locals call it the Grand Canyon of Minnesota. The trolley ride ends in Glen, and with the aid of a large number of talented reenactors, you can step back in time and into the life of an Iron Ranger.

Age of grandchild: 3 and up

Best season: Summer

Contact: Ironworld Discovery Center, 801 Southwest Highway 169, Suite 1, Chisholm, MN 55719 • (800) 372-6437
marketing@ironworld.com • www.ironworld.com

Also check out:

Hill Annex Mine State Park, Calumet; (218) 247-7215; www.dnr.state.mn.us/state_parks/hill_annex_mine

Minnesota Museum of Mining, Chisholm; (218) 254-5543; www.irontrail.org/attractions/mining/mining-museum

Soudan Underground Mine State Park, Soudan; (218) 753-2245 www.dnr.state.mn.us/state_parks/soudan_underground_mine

Grandparents are similar to a piece of string—handy to have around and easily wrapped around the fingers of their grandchildren. Unknown

International Wolf Center

Wolves have a bad reputation, especially with children. This is in large part due to fairy-tales like *Little Red Riding Hood* and *The Three Little Pigs*. But wolves are not villains, nor are they cartoons. Wolves are fascinating creatures that deserve to be observed and understood. The International Wolf Center provides a place for grandparents and grandchildren to do both.

Located in Ely, the center is a natural gateway to the wilderness. Here, your grandchild and you have a wonderful opportunity to connect with wolves—regardless of whether you're a wolf lover or a skeptic.

The most publicized exhibit in the facility is a lifelike display of mounted wolves at a kill site. It was developed by the Science Museum of Minnesota

and was so popular that it traveled around the world before finding a permanent home in Ely, at the edge of the Boundary Waters. The exhibit is loaded with information and graphics. You and your grandchild will see wolves feeding, as well as responding to one another and exhibiting a variety of natural behaviors.

You can also visit the auditorium, which frequently features films and guest speakers. Next it's a stop at the children's room, otherwise known as the wolf den. Inside, your grandchild will be engaged in art and other types of hands-on learning.

However, the main attraction—the exhibit that captures your immediate attention—is the live wolf display. Your grandchild will be awestruck as he watches the real animals and observes their behaviors. He'll hear the wolves howl and perhaps look into a wolf's eyes, seeing it not as a storybook villain but as another life form that deserves its place in nature.

For a truly one-of-a-kind experience, consider planning an excursion with the center's staff on dog sleds or on a howling trip. This requires an extended stay at the facility, but it's well worth it. For your grandchild, it's an opportunity for the exhibits to spill out the doors and into the surrounding woods.

Afterward you can ask him, "Are wolves bad?" Hopefully his experiences at the International Wolf Center will lead him to answer, "No."

Bonding and bridging:

The role of the predator is a difficult one for most adults to understand, let alone kids. Predators are messy eaters—but only because they lack the butcher, knives and forks. The wolf cannot raise chickens, cows, pigs and lambs, but it does help us to control the population of animals like deer, beaver and moose.

Are wolves bad because they eat other living creatures? (I hope not, because we humans do it too.) Does nature even distinguish between good and evil? These are important questions to pose, especially for a grandchild who may see wolves—or other animals—as "bad guys."

A word to the wise:

Your grandchild will be fascinated by the chart that shows the development of the dog varieties. Isn't it amazing to think that the Dachshund, German Shepard, Boxer and Husky are all equally wolves? This chart brings the wolf/human relationship full circle. We have long feared and reviled the wild wolf, but we celebrate, cuddle and extol our beloved dogs. How can it be that they are actually the same animal?

Age of grandchild: 5 and up

Best season: Summer

Contact: International Wolf Center: Teaching the World About Wolves, 1396 Highway 169, Ely, MN 55731 • (218) 365-4695 office2@wolf.org • www.wolf.org

Also check out:

Como Park Zoo and Conservatory, St. Paul; (651) 487-8200; www.comozooconservatory.org

Minnesota Zoo, Apple Valley; (800) 366-7811, www.mnzoo.org

Wildlife Science Center, Forest Lake; (651) 464-3993; www.wildlifesciencecenter.org

Boundary Waters
Canoe Area Wilderness

The Boundary Waters Canoe Area Wilderness is the largest wilderness east of the Rocky Mountains, and it is perhaps the most beloved. Here more than a thousand pristine lakes are connected by trails, and the area features scenic campsites, fishing, swimming, loon and wolf choruses, and a rare chance to feel solitude, silence and privacy. This is a place where you and your grandchild can truly come together.

Forget the more traditional sense of camping. You won't need to carry all of your groceries, sleeping bags, tents and other gear in a backpack while trekking over rugged terrain. (But if you choose to do so, there certainly are opportunities.) Instead, the canoe takes care of that for you. Inside a canoe, two paddlers can balance one another's strengths, converse quietly, set a comfortable pace and let the boat support the weight of your supplies.

Choose your lakes wisely, though. There are potentially some large and difficult portages. Plus, you'll likely want to avoid the worst bug times. You can choose your own route, as long as you apply for a permit soon enough.

Explore the lakes, but be sure to find your campsite early in the day. Start a nice fire, share stories, and go fishing. This is your alone time together, and it's like no time you'll ever be able to share again. Cherish it.

Work together, and teach your grandchild all of the tricks of camping. She may want to return one day with children or grandchildren of her own. Hike into the woods, eat some good campfire food, and look at the stars.

Remember that most children love swimming, so give your grandchild a chance to float in her life jacket. For you, this is a time to relax and settle in. Point out the beauty of the world around you, and let the child develop a sense of the place. Allow her the chance to draw, paint, write or photograph. Encourage her observations, and you'll create in her a true connection with the Boundary Waters.

Sadly the trip must end, but this is time shared that neither of you will ever forget. Together, you journeyed into a wilderness untouched by human hands. You relied on each other completely, and you are much closer for it.

Bonding and bridging:

There's nowhere else in Minnesota like the Boundary Waters Canoe Area Wilderness, and there's no bonding experience that can match it either. This is where your grandchild learns teamwork. It takes both of you to paddle and both of you to portage. Neither one of you can do it alone.

You've put your complete trust in each other, far away from civilization. You're relying on one another, and your grandchild has only you for support. That's something very special to share, and it's an experience that could change your relationship forever.

A word to the wise:

On a very calm evening, put on the life jackets and float your canoe out to where you can watch the sun fall and the stars rise. This is an event that every grandparent and grandchild should share. As you paddle back to land, enjoy the stars reflecting on the water.

Age of grandchild: 10 and up

Best season: Late summer and early fall

Contact: For general information including permits, regulations and planning, visit the Boundary Waters Canoe Area Wilderness website at www.bwcaw.org

Also check out:

Boundary Waters Canoe Area Outfitters; www.bwca.cc

Canoe Country (information); www.canoecountry.com

If a child is to keep alive his inborn sense of wonder, he needs the companionship of at least one adult who can share it, rediscovering with him the joy, excitement and mystery of the world we live in. Rachel Carson

Minnesota's State Parks

We say without hesitation that Minnesota is blessed with the best state park system in the nation. They are in every corner of the state and include history, scenic beauty, spectacular locations and simple places of rest and relaxation. The state parks are some of the greatest resources available to us.

It began with Itasca State Park, which almost became a national park. With 32,000 acres set aside to commemorate the great Mississippi River and to protect the pines, the lakes and the mixed natural communities, this park is the keystone of the system and worth many visits.

It is not the only one. Minnesota's seventy-two state parks represent all three biomes: deciduous, coniferous and prairie. There are jewels along the Mississippi, Red, St. Croix and Minnesota rivers and on the shores of Lake Superior. The parks encompass forts and lighthouses, old mills and ghost towns; more importantly, they encompass our heritage.

Here is a sample of the state-park activities that you and your grandchild can enjoy:

- Quiet picnic grounds in Blue Mounds State Park
- Deep gorges in Banning and Interstate
- Roaring waterfalls in Tettegouche, Gooseberry and Temperance
- Complex rapids in Jay Cooke
- Tall pines in Scenic and Itasca
- Shorelines on large lakes in Zippel Bay and Father Hennepin
- Mining history in Hill Annex and Soudan Underground Mine

Trails, bird watching, flowers, picnics, canoes, fish and relaxation—you'll find it all in Minnesota's state parks, and there is a park within one hour of every person in the state! When should you visit? There is never a bad time. Take your grandchild snowshoeing, hiking, paddling and picnicking, or enjoy the fall leaves/spring flowers.

Bonding and bridging:

Why do we need our state parks? Why does Minnesota set aside some of the region's most breathtaking, beautiful land for public use? The answer, of course, is because we need it. People use these areas to escape from their hectic city lives. Many find spending time in nature to be a spiritual, rejuvenating experience. Therefore, it is important to conserve this land, so everyone has a chance to share it and to enjoy it. Teach your grandchild about the importance that Minnesota's state parks have in your life. Help him to understand why this land is special to you personally. By doing so, you may foster in him a love of nature and an environmental consciousness.

A word to the wise:

Help your grandchild earn patches and certificates by completing activity books designed by state park naturalists. There is one for each of the major biomes: prairie, deciduous and coniferous. The activities are designed to help children learn about plants and animals and will give them useful tips on observing wildlife and enjoying the rich natural world of the state park. Activity books are available at state park offices or visitor centers.

Age of grandchild: All

Best season: All

Contact: Minnesota DNR Information Center, 500 Lafayette Road,
St. Paul, MN 55155 • (888) 646-6367 • www.dnr.state.mn.us/state_parks

Also check out:

Grand Portage National Monument, Grand Portage;
(218) 475-2202; www.nps.gov/grpo

St. Croix National Scenic Riverway, Pine City;
(320) 629-2148 (Marshland Environmental Education Center);
www.nps.gov/sacn

Voyageurs National Park, International Falls;
(218) 283-9821; www.voyageurs.national-park.com

The human spirit needs places where nature has not been rearranged by the hand of man. UNKNOWN

Dog Sledding or Skijoring

What could be better than a mix of snow, children and dogs? Dog sledding and skijoring have long and practical histories. The first dog sledders didn't do it for pleasure; they did it because it was a necessary form of transportation. Lucky for us, it happens to be a lot of fun too!

Dog sledding may not be something that everyone can try, but you and your grandchild will certainly enjoy watching a good dog sled race. The John Beargrease Sled Dog Marathon, held every January, starts in Duluth (weather permitting) and ends in Grand Marais. Bring your grandchild to watch the start, finish and even segments in between. There is great excitement in the air as the dogs bark, yip and pull at their traces in anticipation of takeoff. Standing in the cold, surrounded by these beautiful, enthusiastic animals, it feels as if you've been transported to a different century.

The race may also create a desire to feel that same thrill and energy from the back of a sled. There are some guiding services in the northern part of the state, most notably in Ely, that provide dog sledding experiences. A few winter festivals may also offer sled dog rides.

Skijoring differs from dog sledding because there are fewer dogs harnessed, and they are attached directly to the belt of a person who skis while the dogs pull. Granted, skijoring is not for everyone, and you shouldn't try it with younger grandchildren. It is something you should attempt only if you and your grandchild are capable cross-country skiers and only if you have medium- to large-sized dogs who listen and obey your commands.

This activity is a lot of hard work—for the dogs and for the humans. But it's also one of our favorite things to do with our dogs, and they love skijoring with us so much that we have to hide the equipment when it's not being used!

Skijoring is an ideal sport for teens, but it is one that requires patience and training as you teach your dogs to stay ahead of you and to stop when told.

Bonding and bridging:

In the old days, sled dogs were whipped, abused and literally worked to death. These are bad memories that we hope will never return. It is up to all of us to treat animals with kindness and compassion, whether we raise them for food, for work or for pleasure.

Sled dogs love their work, as long as they are loved. As grandparents and grandchildren, we must respect the animal kingdom. Doing so improves our environment and makes us happier, better people.

A word to the wise:

The John Beargrease Sled Dog Marathon is a wonderful event to watch. The excitement of the animals transfers to the spectators; the elements of the landscape blend to create a beautiful mental image. Who cares who wins? Just let yourself slip into the energy of this powerful event.

Age of grandchild: 8 and up for dog sleds, 10 and up for skijoring

Best season: Winter

Contact: The John Beargrease Sled Dog Marathon,
PO Box 500, Duluth, MN 55801 • (218) 722-7631
info@beargrease.com • www.beargrease.com

Also check out:

Paul Schurke's Wintergreen Dog Sledding Vacations, Ely;
(218) 365-6022; www.dogsledding.com

White Wilderness Sled Dog Adventures, Ely;
(800) 701-6238; www.whitewilderness.com

Wild Institute's women's sled dog trips, Loretto;
(763) 479-3954; www.thewildinstitute.com

It's funny what happens when you become a grandparent. You start to act all goofy and do things you never thought you'd do. It's terrific. MIKE KRZYZEWSKI

113

Kayak Race

In the Land of Ten Thousand Lakes we sometimes forget the wonderful rivers that served as the state's original highways. Canoes, portages, Voyageurs and heavy packs are part of the legacy. But, in fact, there is another combination that is much more prevalent today: the kayak, the double-bladed paddle, the rivers' turbulent rapids and no portage allowed!

Kayak races are a wonderful combination of human skill and the power of water passing through rocky canyons, over waterfalls and around rocks. The kayaks are colorful plastics, the paddlers wear a mix of hues, and the scenery is the kind that people travel hundreds of miles to explore and photograph.

Spectators watch from bridges and rocky cliffs trying to glimpse the brave kayakers, who are working in water that no one could swim, fighting currents to avoid obstacles and traveling the rough waves without being washed downstream.

The race is not just a speed event from start to finish. Officials hang gates that each kayak must pass through. Plus, you can bet the judges have chosen a challenging route.

Be sure to point out the variations in the river flow and how the talented paddler can use the current to her advantage. Maybe there is a lesson for all of us in this: We must learn to enjoy and work with nature. We can watch the athletes and know that they succeed by cooperating with nature, yet they will never conquer its forces.

Kayak races are a part of the Olympics, but most people have yet to discover how fun it can be to experience nature and athleticism in the same setting. The crowds are small, the excitement is high, and the view is spectacular.

Spending time outdoors with your grandchild and watching athletes who don't keep score but rather participate for the love of kayaking, that's a great way to spend an afternoon.

Bonding and bridging:

A kayak race is the place where you can revel in the accomplishments of individuals who compete (often against only themselves and the river) without million-dollar contracts and TV incentives. These people set goals and work hard to achieve them.

Ask your grandchild what her goals and dreams are? If she does not have any, spend time creating some with her, and be sure to write them down. (Goals should pose a challenge but should not be impossible to attain.) Next, ask her what she's doing to reach her goals. Help her to formulate a plan for success, and encourage her to achieve more than she dreamed possible.

A word to the wise:

The sea kayak is another type of kayak that's colorful and fun. This versatile boat might be ideal for camping and exploring, but the city of Two Harbors has also found it to be a popular sports vehicle and the center of another festival. The first weekend in August brings boaters and spectators together for the Two Harbors Kayak Festival, featuring music, kids' paddling and a variety of options for competition. Visit www.kayakfestival.org.

Age of grandchild: 10 and up

Best season: Summer

Contact: Rec Sports Outdoor Program
(University of Minnesota), Duluth, MN 55812
(218) 726-7128 • rsop@d.umn.edu • www.umdrsop.org

Also check out:

July: North Shore Dragonboat Festival, Grand Marais;
(218) 387-2372; www.northshoredragonboat.com

August: Mississippi River Challenge from Coon Rapids Dam,
Coon Rapids; (651) 222-2193 (Friends of the Mississippi River);
www.mississippiriverchallenge.org

Railroad Ride

Your grandchild has probably been watching cartoon versions of trains on television, in books and perhaps even has a few toy trains. For you, railroads are nostalgic. You remember a time when railroads were more prevalent in our lives. Therefore, a railroad ride means something different to both of you. You will share the experience, but your adventures will be on different levels.

The excitement begins at the ticket window. By the time you line up to get on board, your grandchild's eyes will be as big as the train's large wheels. He'll look up to see the engineer, get anxious as you approach the conductor and excitedly jump into the train, as you race to find the seats that you want.

A railroad train is not an amusement ride; there is no surge of adrenaline. Instead it is a relaxing journey. You may even remember tales of your old rail journeys or of the electric train set you used to play with.

Railroad cars have many windows, and you should put your grandchild beside one. Settle in and wait for the whistle. Next comes the surge as the cars remove the slack between them, and finally the train begins to move.

Look out the windows, and walk among the moving cars. If you can, talk to the conductor: His uniform may as well be a superhero outfit for your grandchild. Pick up a few postcards, so the child can write one for his mom and dad that tells about your trip. Bring along a snack for later in the ride too.

Minnesota has some great options for train rides. For instance, you can hop aboard the North Shore Railroad at the Depot in Duluth or catch a ride on the Zephyr in Stillwater. You can plan your trip around special events like a visit from Thomas the Tank Engine or a pizza train. Check into it, and see which ride is best for you and your grandchild.

Best of all, you don't have to concentrate on the wheel, the gas and other drivers. You can truly relax and share the time with your little partner.

Bonding and bridging:

Trains are an important part of our everyday lives, one that we almost never think about—unless we get stuck behind one! But what would our lives be like without trains? For one thing, much of what we purchase would cost a great deal more. (Freight trains are an economical means of transporting goods, which helps keep prices down.)

There are plenty of things in your grandchild's life that he may not like but which serve a greater purpose. He probably doesn't appreciate all of his classes in school, but each is taught for a reason. He may have rules to follow or chores to do at home, which are in place to keep him safe and to teach him important values. Talk to your grandchild about the aspects of his life that he dislikes. Explain to him why things are the way they are, and help him understand. Generally speaking, if we adults took the time to explain why, we'd have much happier children.

A word to the wise:

For a little extra magic during the holiday season, Stillwater's Minnesota Zephyr brings the excitement of *The Polar Express* to life. This classic children's book (and now a movie) is a holiday favorite, and you can give your grandchild the thrill of a lifetime. The forty-five-minute trip includes a box lunch, snacks, strolling carolers and—of course—a visit with Santa Claus!

Age of grandchild: 2 to 10

Best season: All

Contact: Minnesota Zephyr, PO Box 573, 601 North Main Street,
Stillwater, MN 55082 • (800) 992-6100 • www.minnesotazephyr.com

Also check out:

Minnesota Railroad Club; www.tc.umn.edu/~rrclubum

Minnesota Railroads; www.dot.state.mn.us/ofrw/railroads.html

North Shore Scenic Railroad, Duluth; (800) 423-1273; www.northshorescenicrailroad.org

Grandparents are made in Heaven, born with the birth of their first grandchild. GAIL LUMET BUCKLEY

The Classic Drive-in

During the 1950s and '60s, drive-ins were the equivalent to today's fast food restaurants; they were convenient and designed for the traveler. However, the comparisons stop there. Drive-ins offered more than simple burgers-and-fries menus, and the food was cooked fresh for each order.

Some of my favorite memories from childhood involve stopping with my parents at the beautiful Frostop drive-in in Taylors Falls. A cold mug of root beer on a tray just outside the window was the most wonderful summer sight imaginable.

As I got older, the drive-in became a place for luxuriating in my car or for sitting at an outside table. We talked to our neighboring car-mates, met friends and spent time there. Fast food? Forget it! When I was in high school, we spent the entire evening at the drive-in with onion rings on our breath.

Nowadays, there aren't many places like the old-fashioned A&W, Frostop and Porky's. Fortunately there are still a few around, and they should be visited for nostalgia and a meal.

How fun it will be for you to bring your grandchild, order from the car and play some '50s music. Tell her how this was part of your travel and social experiences. Sip that big mug of root beer, and talk about how everything is different.

Compare today's fast-food restaurants with the drive-in. It might even be fun to play a recording of an old *The Shadow* radio program or something else that you may have enjoyed.

This opportunity to reminisce is sure to make an impression on any grandchild. The chance to share a frosty mug and a delicious meal together is an added bonus.

Bonding and bridging:

My, how times have changed. Remember when we were young? We used to go to a drive-in to spend time. Nowadays, people go through the drive-through to save time!

There is one very simple, very important message that comes with a trip to an old-fashioned drive-in: Stop and smell the roses. Don't be in such a rush. Take time to enjoy what life has to offer. A good meal is something that should be savored and shared with others. It should not be scarfed down, in your car, while you're on the way home from the grocery store.

Your grandchild will be fascinated to hear about the good ol' days, when you were a teenager. Seize this opportunity to teach her a little about taking time to appreciate the world around her.

A word to the wise:

Stay outside. Be sure to order and eat from your car, rather than going into the restaurant. Doing so will give your grandchild the unique feeling of the '50s drive-in. If you can, have her parents come in a separate car and park next to you, so you can chit-chat back and forth, just like we used to do.

Age of grandchild: All

Best season: Summer

Contact: The Drive-in (Frostop), 527 Bench Street, Taylors Falls, MN 55084
(651) 465-7831 • www.taylorsfalls.com/drivein.html

Also check out:

A&W, Pine City, Nisswa, Park Rapids and Duluth; www.awrestaurants.com

Porky's, St. Paul; (651) 644-1790

It is not a slight thing when they who are so fresh from God, love us. CHARLES DICKENS

Ice Cream Cones

It's a hot day, humidity in the air. What's first aid for too much summer? Quick! Get that grandchild an ice cream cone.

Eating an ice cream cone can be done in many places and in many forms. At one time ice cream was cold, smooth, solid and soft enough to scoop but not runny enough to flow out of a machine. Then Dairy Queen came, and our perceptions changed. Now we have ice cream and soft serve.

Since we are looking for places and experiences that stand out, we favor the local establishments over the franchises. A great place to go for a "neighborhood" atmosphere is Conny's Creamy Cones on Maryland and Dale in St. Paul. It is a walk-up palace of frozen delights. Conny's specialty is blending flavors into their soft serve, giving your grandchild and you any of dozens of flavors prepared especially for you.

Another local favorite, Sebastian Joe's consistently gets votes for the best ice cream in the Twin Cities. The flavors are rich and full—forget subtlety. Plus most flavors are not on other ice cream boards. It is family-owned, and it specializes in both unique flavors and good ingredients. The vanilla is blended with ground beans rather than extract, and every other flavor maintains the same quality. Stop with your grandchild at either of the two stores: One is located on Franklin one block off Hennepin in Minneapolis, and the other is in the Linden Hills area near Lake Harriet.

In St. Paul, Grand Ole Creamery on Grand Avenue is an old-fashioned scoop joint: not a lot of atmosphere but plenty of good ice cream. Do you know how the cone always softens as you eat the ice cream, and ultimately the bottom becomes a hose of liquid running down your chin and shirt? Well, Grand Ole Creamery has a solution. A malted milk ball is placed in the bottom of the cone, a welcome treat and a plug to stop the leak.

At Izzy's in St. Paul, you can appreciate the installed solar panels that produce the electricity needed to cool the ice cream. Innovation and fun are part of the attraction at this local establishment that was listed as one of the hundred best places in America.

Bonding and bridging:

Almost everyone remembers a grandparent taking him out for an ice cream cone. For the young, this is a magical experience. Sitting, dribbling and talking is as good as it gets. Eating ice cream is a time when it's okay to spill, and getting messy is half the fun. Set an example here that life isn't always about being neat, tidy and orderly. Once in a while, getting down and dirty is just fine. In fact, it can be a lot of fun!

A word to the wise:

Raspberry Chocolate Chip is the highest-rated flavor at Sebastian Joe's, and it must be tasted. The homemade waffle cones at Grand Ole Creamery are almost as good as the ice cream that goes in them. At Izzy's you can try the Izzy Scoop: At no extra charge, you choose from a variety of special flavors for a small scoop on top of your cone. It is a great way to sample a new flavor, and everyone likes something free—especially when it's so delicious.

Age of grandchild: All

Best season: Summer

Contact:

Conny's Creamy Cones, 1197 Dale Street North, St. Paul, MN 55117

Grand Ole Creamery, 750 Grand Avenue, St. Paul, MN 55105
www.grandolecreamery.com

Izzy's Ice Cream Café, 2034 Marshall Avenue, St. Paul, MN 55104
www.izzysicecream.com

Sebastian Joe's, 1007 West Franklin Avenue, Minneapolis, MN 55405

Sebastian Joe's, 4321 Upton Avenue South, Minneapolis, MN 55410

Also check out:

Pumphouse Creamery, 4754 Chicago Avenue, Minneapolis, MN 55407

Sonny's Ice Cream, 3401 Lyndale Avenue South, Minneapolis, MN 55408

Paddlewheel Ride

Rivers were our original highways, and paddlewheels served as a river's version of a cruise ship. It was the primary means for moving people and goods and for entertainment. These colorful vessels, with their large rotating blades churning the river waters, created a melody to which people traveled.

The paddlewheel was a floating palace. Strangers came from near and far to be a part of the colorful boats that featured organ music and minstrel shows. It was a river circus. No wonder Mark Twain was so inspired. Living along the Mississippi, he must have watched these boats like today's Minnesota children look at new cars and motorcycles, trains and airplanes.

Boarding a paddlewheel is like entering a floating mansion. Excitement comes from the fact that this does not look like a boat. It looks like a hotel. You can lead your grandchild across the gangplank and enter a new landscape. Don't be in a rush to go inside the boat. Take a walk around the deck. Let your grandchild see the ornate trim and the detailed painting. Stroll to the wheel at the boat's rear. This is a good place to be when the boat takes off. Try to anticipate when the blades will start moving, and watch as they grab the water and roll over, pulling the heavy boat backward or pushing it forward.

Once the paddlewheel is underway, stroll through the elaborate interior. Climb to the upper deck, and watch the scenery from the top for a while. These are tall boats, and the view is grand. Up here you might be able to see the pilot's cabin (wheelhouse) too.

Finally, go inside to enjoy the food and the lively entertainment.

We have very few interactions with rivers in our everyday lives, yet these ancient pathways are still important to migrating animals and to commerce. It is good for us to introduce children to the idea of the river and the free flow of water that connects us with the sea.

Bonding and bridging:

Sure, you could take a speedboat across the Mississippi River, but what fun would that be? The old paddlewheel is a prime example that slow beats fast any day. I don't need a thrill-a-minute, adrenaline-rush powerboat. Give me a quiet, relaxing, laid-back journey. I like to have time to take in the scenery. But this is where a gap in generational values is apparent. Our task as grandparents is to teach our grandchildren that there's more to life than fast-moving vehicles. Sometimes it's far better to enjoy the trip than it is to arrive at the destination.

A word to the wise:

Live entertainment has always been a riverboat tradition, and you can still experience this thrill with your grandchild today. On some of the St. Paul cruises, you can enjoy a delicious meal and a wonderful theatrical production. During special Stillwater cruises, your meal comes complete with some good old-fashioned music, performed by a dixieland band. This is definitely the way to travel!

Age of grandchild: 2 and up

Best season: Fall

Contact: St. Croix Boat & Packet Company, 525 Main Street,
Stillwater, MN 55082 • (651) 430-1234
postmaster@andiamo-ent.com • www.andiamo-ent.com

Also check out:

Minneapolis Queen (Boom Island), Minneapolis; (888) 791-6220; www.minneapolisqueen.com

Padelford Packet Boats Company, Incorporated, St. Paul; (651) 227-1100; www.riverrides.com

Taylors Falls Scenic Boat Tours, Taylors Falls; (800) 447-4958; www.wildmountain.com

They say genes skip generations. Maybe that's why grandparents find their grandchildren so likeable. Joan McIntosh

County Fair

Sure, you should go to the State Fair, but don't judge all fairs by that standard. County fairs cost less, are less intense and are more expressive of Americana. At a rural county fair, we see neighbors gather, talk, laugh and enjoy themselves. It is a place for your neighbor's child to win a ribbon and for your friend to show her sheep.

Start the trip by bringing your grandkid to the petting zoo. Kids love animals, and the chance to pet bunnies, lambs and puppies is a dream come true. Next it's off to the 4-H building and livestock barns. Show her the blue-ribbon animals and snap some photos. (Remember to have your grandchild wash her hands when she is finished.)

After that, it's off to the midway for some thrills. Be selective in which rides you let the grandchild choose, and you may even want to join her on one or two. The Ferris wheel is a must if you can take the heights. From the top, your grandchild can see the entire fairgrounds, pointing out where she's already been and where she still wants to go.

A few games are fun too, but don't waste too much money trying to win impossible prizes. Instead, it's better to buy your grandchild a small souvenir.

Finally, it's time to eat! Feed her all of her favorite fair foods. Mini donuts mix with burritos, french fries, lemonade, milk stands and hot dogs. You definitely want to save this for last because it's the best part. Plus, fair food before fair rides often makes for sick grandchildren!

If you're visiting at the right time, usually in the evenings, remember the tractor pulls and car races at the grandstand. Those can be a lot of fun, but don't expect to stay for the whole thing. A grandchild may get bored after a while.

Overall, a county fair offers a variety of things to do and is not to be missed. You can dunk a neighbor, win a ribbon and eat cotton candy. Bands play, the crowd buzzes and the loudspeakers blare. Is this innocence? Is this the simple life? It is a place that the State Fair can only hope to replicate in little doses.

Bonding and bridging:

Think back to when we were young. What was the purpose of a county fair? Of course, it was about having fun. But it was more than that. It was a time for farmers to stop harvesting in order to come into town. It was a time when stores closed and an entire county set aside its busy schedules for a chance to come together.

Times have changed, and that meaning has been lost in the mix of thrill rides and high-priced food. But there's still something special about a county fair. It's a celebration, with fun at every turn. Be sure to remind your grandchild what the greater purpose of the county fair used to be. Especially as children get older and grow into adulthood, setting aside time for fun, family and the community becomes increasingly important.

A word to the wise:

The Carlton County Fair has one extra flair: It is held on the same fair-grounds that house their old pioneer buildings. It is history and the present in one colossal combination. I suspect that many children will reflect, if asked, on how fun the fair was and how different it was from other fairs. The grandstand events include horse racing, car racing and a dog show.

Age of grandchild: All

Best season: The Carlton County fair is in mid-August. (Other county fairs are held throughout the summer months.)

Contact: Minnesota Federation of County Fairs; www.mfcf.com

Also check out:

Explore Minnesota Tourism; (888) 868-7476; www.exploreminnesota.com

Minnesota State Fair, St. Paul; (651) 288-4400; www.mnstatefair.org

Pow Wow

No one knows how pow wows began, although there are many theories. The word "pow wow" is believed to be from the Narrganseet Tribe, referring to a curing ceremony. Some think that pow wows were started by the war dance society of the Ponca. The First Nation in Canada website says, "Songs and dances that signified spirituality and religion were used in ceremonies. Upon seeing these ceremonies, the early European explorers thought pow wow was the whole dance when it actually referred to healers and spiritual leaders by the Algonkian phrase *Pau Wau.*"

I am filled with pleasure at a pow wow. Here I see happiness displayed in dance and music, conversation and action. Native costumes are worn as an expression of continuity and promise. There is no replacing the experience. For your grandchild and you, attending a pow wow is like being transported to another world.

Pow wows consist of social dances that have special meanings for the nations and their histories. From the very beginning, your grandchild will be captivated. As the Grand Entry opens the pow wow, the eagle staff leads a flag procession (of the tribal nation, the United States, POWs and the military) carried with great reverence. The flags are followed by the dancers, first the men then the women.

The intensity of a pow wow is unmatched. It's almost tangible. Your grandchild will feel the drum beat and may even get a sense of traveling back in time, as the music combines history, religion and social norms. The singers are important members of the American Indian society; the drums are sacred and passed on to each generation. Old songs are mixed with new songs, elders sit beside youth at the drums, and the dance includes participants of all ages and genders. Some feel that the drum is the heartbeat, an answer to the vibration of the Creator's first thoughts as the world was created.

Every part of the pow wow is done in a sacred circle that is inclusive and represents the circle of life. Veterans, elders, princesses and organizers are all honored, and everyone is made to feel welcome. A pow wow is one experience that your grandchild and you will never forget.

Bonding and bridging:

The United States is known as the "melting pot" for good reason. Our country is made of diverse people from varying cultures and with different backgrounds. A pow wow is an excellent chance to expose your grandchild to the traditions of another ethnic group. Here you can watch these proud people celebrating their cultural identity.

Ask your grandchild what he thinks his identity is. (This may be a tough concept, so be ready with examples.) Ask him what traditions he celebrates. Holidays? Vacations? Family reunions? Share with him the importance of tradition in honoring your ancestors. It is a time to celebrate with loved ones, while remembering those who came before us—who helped shape the world we live in and the people we are today.

A word to the wise:

The Mille Lacs Band of Ojibwe has held its pow wow annually since 1965. Located in a wooded area with a bay of Mille Lacs Lake as its backdrop, the setting adds to the event and provides the right feeling for fun and reflection. To make the event perfect, get some fresh Fry Bread and an Indian Taco.

Age of grandchild: 2 and up

Best season: The Mille Lacs Band of Ojibwe pow wow is held during the third weekend of August. (In general, pow wows take place throughout the year; they are held inside during winter.)

Contact: The Mille Lacs Band of Ojibwe pow wow is twelve miles north of Onamia • (320) 532-7496 • www.millelacsojibwe.org

Also check out:

These locations also host pow wows throughout the year: Bemidji, Cass Lake, Grand Portage, Granite Falls, Hastings, Hinckley, Leech Lake, Mahnomen, Mankato, Marshall, Mendota, Minneapolis (Heart of the Earth), Red Lake, Robbinsdale, Shakopee, St. Paul and Warroad

For more information, visit these websites:
- www.powwows.com
- www.drumhop.com

Folk or Ethnic Music Festival

How do we introduce children to music? Do we simply turn on the radio and hope for the best, or do we wait until they are influenced by their peers, investing in a form of music based on pressure rather than choice?

Music is a basic part of our human experience. We have ethnic music because music is inherent to all cultures and to all countries. It is a sense of rhythm which allows us to walk and run, and which we use as a form of personal expression.

When a child is young, she is not prejudiced to a form or style; she is simply moved by the beat and excitement of sound and structure. Research has shown that a child's ability to hear and sort the complex aspects of music develops the brain for complex thinking in other areas of learning and development. Music has value for contemplation and for individual experience, but music can also be a strong social bonding tool.

I advocate taking your grandchild to a folk or ethnic music festival (which are often combined) because of the positive qualities of the experience. The music is rhythmic and basic, with varieties of unique instruments—from bagpipes to dulcimers—that will not be heard in the normal guitar/bass/piano mix in most forms of popular music.

You can also visit a rock, country or blues festival, or any other type of music event, but the questions that should be asked are

- Is the music, including the language, appropriate?

- Will there be drinking and rowdiness that could intimidate children or make them uncomfortable?

- Is the event kid-friendly? Will children need to remain too quiet and keep too still?

In our experience, the folk/ethnic music venue meets all of the criteria and provides a great event for listeners from multiple generations.

Bonding and bridging:

Music is a unique form of communication and expression: It is the international language. In fact, many generations can be better understood simply by studying the music. From Civil War songs such as *Battle Hymn of the Republic* to the music of the Civil Rights Movement including *We Shall Overcome*—and even the controversies surrounding Elvis Presley in the 1960s and gangsta rap today—music tells us a great deal about the identities of each era.

Ask your grandchild what kind of music she enjoys. Ask her what songs she thinks will define her generation. By considering music and its impact on society, she will open the door to creative ways of thinking and to a greater appreciation of the arts.

A word to the wise:

Try to attend a festival that includes dancing. The movement of the dancers, the costumes and the choreography are unique and enticing. From clog dancing to ceili dancing, each form of ethnic and folk dancing is captivating.

Age of grandchild: All

Best season: Summer

Contact: Minnesota Folk Festival, 626 Armstrong Avenue, St. Paul, MN 55102 • mnfolkfestival@aol.com www.minnesotafolkfestival.org

Also check out:

May: Festival of Nations, St. Paul; www.festivalofnations.com

June: Nisswa-Stamman Nordic Folk Music Festival, Nisswa; www.nisswastamman.org

July: Chief O'Neill Day, Hastings; www.minnesotafolkfestival.org

August: Minnesota Irish Fair, St. Paul; www.irishfair.com

Children have never been very good at listening to their elders, but they have never failed to imitate them. James Baldwin

Miniature Golf

When I was young, we used to hang out at a Putt Putt golf course. We'd laugh, compete or just relax among friends. Today's miniature golf courses are much different. In fact, they've almost become small amusement parks! But the simplicity of the game remains the same, and it is worth sharing with your grandchild.

The object of miniature golf is pretty straightforward: Hit the ball from the pad at the beginning and make it into the hole in as few tries as possible. Of course, you may have to go up and down, through a windmill, around a corner and over some water.

Tell your grandchild that the trick to having a good time is not to think of miniature golf as a competitive sport. Rather, he should look at each hole as a small stage, and the golf ball is the vehicle that must travel through the course and into the "garage" (or hole). It's best if you don't bother keeping score or declaring a winner.

As a grandparent, keep in mind that you have only two objectives: Help your grandchild with his hand/eye coordination and teach him how to play. When we share, we bond and we learn. It is a simple process, but it can get lost if we let our competitive spirits overwhelm our fun and recreation.

Another thrill of the game is discovering what crazy obstacles each course offers. There is so much variety between the many courses that you never know what you'll come across next. Tall waterfalls, animals, houses and more create a fantasy-land that pleasantly enhances your grandchild's experience. Many places even find ways to teach subtle lessons or highlight certain themes with their course décor. One such place is the bright and creative Pirate's Cove in Brainerd, featuring two eighteen-hole landscapes. You can find many other excellent miniature golf courses throughout the state.

Miniature golf is an example of a game that can be fun, relaxing and laid back. It has the extra attraction of being colorful and imaginative, but even more importantly it's a fun activity that we can share with our grandchildren.

Bonding and bridging:

Miniature golf is fun, but playing a round is about more than having a good time. It's important for your grandchild to observe you in a competitive situation. What you say and how you act will set the tone for this day of recreation and for your grandchild's future activities—sports, spelling bees, board games and so on.

Model for him an attitude that is more about having fun and less about winning. You must set an example of a person who emphasizes good sportsmanship and fair play. Do that, and he will do you proud as he gets older.

A word to the wise:

The miniature golf course at the Science Museum of Minnesota is like no other. Several exhibits are connected to the golf course, providing plenty of opportunities for your grandchild to learn while he plays. Plus, there is a maze next to the course—a fun place to wander and enjoy before or after your round of mini golf.

Age of grandchild: 5 and up

Best season: Summer

Contact: The Science Museum of Minnesota,
120 West Kellogg Boulevard, St. Paul, MN 55102
(800) 221-9444 • www.smm.org/bigbackyard/top.php

Also check out:

L.A.R.K. Toy Store, Kellogg; (507) 767-3387; www.larktoys.com

Pirate's Cove, Brainerd; (218) 828-9002; www.piratescove.net

Putt'er There Mini Golf, Como Park Zoo, St. Paul; (651) 487-8200;
www.comozooconservatory.org/cons/amenities/minigolf.shtml

Each day of our lives we make deposits in the memory banks of our children. CHARLES R. SWINDOLL

Fireworks

There is something exciting about a fireworks show that is hard to find in any other shared adventure with your grandchild. You are letting her stay up late, you are taking her into a dark night, and you are watching an aerial display that is colorful, loud and unusual.

Fireworks supposedly date back more than two thousand years, and some say they were the result of an accident in a kitchen. However, it was the Italians who perfected the idea of colored sparks lighting the night sky.

Minnesota has plenty of options for fireworks, from the Winter Carnival to the Aquatennial. Almost every town has a fair, and the Fourth of July just can't be celebrated without the explosions and colors of a good fireworks show. But if you can only watch one, the State Fair features the granddaddy of all Minnesota pyrotechnics.

In some ways, an evening of fireworks is a perfect opportunity to remove some of a grandchild's fear of the dark. A warm summer evening, a blanket spread on the grass, a thermos of hot cocoa and you are ready. You build the image that you want to place in your grandchild's memory. Here is comfort in the night.

There is always a lot of waiting and anticipating at these events: waiting for enough darkness, waiting while the crew prepares and waiting for the next explosion of light. Will it be a dud, or will it be the best one of the night?

Remember that most children are not used to being up this late, and they do not know how dangerous fireworks can be. Give your grandchild some safety tips in a positive environment. As she grows older, her fascination with fireworks and gunpowder will change. How you handle these topics now could be important in her future.

Share your wisdom, but also allow her imagination to soar. Let her "oooh" and "ahhhh" along with you—what fun!

Bonding and bridging:

People of all ages are fascinated by a good fire-works display. It is the sheer awe of color, light and sound in the night sky. There could be lessons here, but sometimes just being together, smiling and having fun are enough.

A word to the wise:

Chanhassen's Fourth of July celebration is a full weekend of fun. From pony rides to a petting zoo, your grandchild is bound to find plenty to keep her entertained. Carnival games, water wars and a kiddie parade just add to the excitement. Stay late for the grand finale: one of the state's best fireworks shows. The fireworks explode into beautiful lights over Lake Ann and are even choreographed to music.

Age of grandchild: All

Best season: Summer

Contact: City of Chanhassen, 7700 Market Boulevard, PO Box 147, Chanhassen, MN 55317 • (952) 227-1100 www.ci.chanhassen.mn.us/parks/july4.html

Also check out:

Most counties offer several opportunities to see a fireworks display. From Memorial Day and Independencee Day to New Year's Eve and various other community festivals, you'll find several occasions for fireworks within driving distance of you. Check your area's community calendars to find a fireworks show near you.

I've learned that when your newly born grandchild holds your little finger in his fist, that you're hooked for life. ANDY ROONEY

Hot Air
Balloon Ride

The sky above doesn't hold as much mystery to our grandchildren as it did for us when we were their age. Children today are growing up with rockets in space, satellites sending photographs from other planets, helicopters zooming overhead and airplane rides to reach far off destinations. Despite all of that, a ride in a hot air balloon inspires imagination and a desire for adventure.

Climbing aboard a hot air balloon is a thrill for you and your grandchild. You can't beat standing inside the giant wicker basket, a colorful balloon rising into the air. You see farm fields and towns, tree tops and rivers. This isn't looking out an airplane window. This is feeling the air on your face, with no barriers between you and the world below.

Hot air balloons are surprisingly loud, so conversation may have to wait until the ride is over. But the noise of the massive heaters does not diminish the feeling of floating and the sense that you are part of the wind, connected to the currents in the air. Unlike any other vehicle, a hot air balloon allows you to adjust height but not direction. Instead, nature decides your destination.

As an added bonus, this is a great way for your grandchild to learn a little about science. Hot air rises and cold air falls. Hot air balloons take advantage of this; they use a burner to blow hot air into the balloon, trapping the heated air and causing it to rise against the cooler air above. The basket, the heater and the riders typically weigh about a thousand pounds, and it takes close to 65,000 cubic feet of heated air to raise that much weight into the air. That's why the balloon is so big and the basket so small.

The thought of riding in a hot air balloon may be a little scary for you and your grandchild. If either of you views it as extremely scary, perhaps you should skip this activity. Your time together should be fun, not traumatic. But if it's just frightening enough where the two of you can overcome your fears, a hot air balloon ride is a thrill that both of you will remember for the rest of your lives.

Bonding and bridging:

As you approach that giant balloon, your heart beats a little faster. Butterflies start flying in your stomach. You may even begin to sweat. Now you're seeing things from your grandchild's perspective.

Especially for younger children, many of the activities in this book are "firsts" for them. A lot of these adventures may even make them nervous. You'll do well to put yourself in your grandchild's place. Remember how it feels to try something foreign and new. That way, you'll be better prepared with a hand around the shoulder or some words of encouragement on your next excursion.

A word to the wise:

Every September, the town of Faribault hosts Airfest and a hot air balloon rally. This brings together ultra-lights, balloons, historical planes and every kind of flying machine imaginable. Think of the colors on all of those balloons rising from the early morning mists. It's quite an experience to share with your grandchild.

Age of grandchild: 10 and up

Best season: Fall

Contact: Faribault Airfest (Faribault Area Chamber of Commerce), Faribault, MN 55021 • (800) 658-2354 • www.faribaultairfest.com

Also check out:

Balloon Ascensions Unlimited, Prior Lake; (952) 447-5677

Balloons at Stillwater, Stillwater; (651) 439-1800

Stardrifter Hot Air Balloons, Mapleton; (507) 245-3844

Steve Johnson Hot Air Balloon, Duluth; (218) 724-3747

Wiederkehr Balloons, Lakeland; (651) 436-8172

We must act as elders of the tribe, looking out for the interests of the future and preserving the precious compact between the generations. MAGGIE KUHN

River Canoeing

Canoeing is about connecting with nature, and nothing beats canoeing as a traditional Minnesota experience. The state is home to the Boundary Waters Canoe Area, the largest canoe wilderness in the world. Plus, you'll find some of the best canoe rivers around.

I did not have the opportunity to explore the wild places when I was a child. But in 1965—as an adult—I journeyed down the Rum River (near Anoka) with a friend. It is not a rough river, but for me it was quite an adventure.

We paddled with no sense of what lay in front of us, so every bend was a surprise: a new vista and an unfolding personal drama. We slid down the river, often moving from one side to the other. We accidentally drifted under a tree filled with starlings. Because we had been quiet, the starlings did not sense us until we were beneath them. They suddenly took flight with a rush of air, and I will never forget the foil-like sound of their wings unfolding and taking the first beat. I have continued pursuing nature's mysteries in all of my decades since that moment.

For your grandchild, a float down a river—seeing birds, watching the landscape, dropping a line in the water and stopping for a swim or a picnic—is a life-changing experience.

Remember to make it fun: Don't plan a trip that's too long, avoid headwinds, bring food and beverages in a cooler, bring protection against biting flies, and

let the grandchild paddle with you. For an ideal experience, choose a wild but flat stream. These are just a few of many great options:

- Cannon River

- St. Croix River (Taylors Falls to Osceola)

- Mississippi River (the source to the Twin Cities)

- Crow Wing River (Stigman's Mound Park to McGivern Park)

Bonding and bridging:

In an age when everything is expected to have a motor, to make noise and to go fast, you can help your grandchild understand that slowing down means experiencing more. Paddle, not to get somewhere, but to be somewhere. The sun, the breeze, the birds, the fish, the horizon and the sunset are what call the canoeist.

A river connects us to the land and to the larger continent. Rivers are big ideas, wild concepts and enormous systems, but they invite us to float and become one with their energies. A river makes you wonder where it comes from and where it's going. To sit beside the river, toss in a few sticks and watch them go is an invitation to speak of bigger issues and to help solve the mysteries that perplex the young mind.

A word to the wise:

If you feel up to it, a camp out on a river trip is one of those very special opportunities to share and bond. A canoe allows you to bring much more than you might if you were backpacking, and it puts you in remote sites where the quiet movement of the water becomes your background noise for setting up camp, making a meal and sitting in front of a fire.

Age of grandchild: 8 and up

Best season: Late spring and early summer (It depends upon the amount of rain that has fallen. Check river levels before setting out.)

Contact: Minnesota DNR (canoeing); www.dnr.state.mn.us/canoeing

Also check out:

Boundary Waters Canoe Area Wilderness; www.bwcaw.org

Minneapolis Chain of Lakes, Minneapolis; www.minneapolisparks.org/grandrounds/dist_cl.htm

It is one of nature's ways that we often feel closer to distant generations than to the generations immediately preceding us. IGOR STRAVINSKY

Snowshoeing

For a lot of people, winter means it's time to seal up the house, gather three months' worth of supplies and hunker down until March. Those people are missing out. The winter months offer countless opportunities for you to share in special activities with your grandchild—like snowshoeing.

Snowshoeing is among the most pleasant and satisfying of winter sports. It gives you freedom of movement, a quiet environment and exercise. Unlike skiing, the skill level needed is low and the cost is quite reasonable. In fact, all you really need is available land that is covered with snow and a couple pairs of snowshoes.

Snowshoeing allows you to take your grandchild through the scenery of your favorite places in a new and refreshing way. You can look for tracks of all the mysterious animals and travelers, and you can follow their stories as you walk along their paths. Snowshoe beside streams if you have the chance; your grandchild will likely find numerous animal tracks there. State park trails are also great to explore.

Keep your trek limited to the daylight hours, and realize that snowshoeing generates a lot of heat. If you dress too warmly you'll sweat, which ultimately chills your body (and you don't want to chill your body if you're outside in the elements during winter).

Bring food, and eat regularly in small stops (so you don't get too cold). Drink plenty of water, and—most importantly—take hikes that are within both your grandchild's range and your own. Snowshoeing should be a fun activity, in which you can be together and share. It should not be a difficult journey for either of you.

Avoid wearing clothes that absorb water, such as jeans. Instead, use wool, synthetics or waterproof clothing, so you can flop in the snow and have fun without getting soaked.

By following these tips, you'll have a wonderful time with your grandchild, and you might even forget that it's still several months until summer.

Bonding and bridging:

Grandchildren will look out the window on a cold winter morning, see the ground covered in a white blanket, and realize that it's time to go out and play. It's not that simple for us grandparents. Sometimes we need an excuse to get outside and have fun, and snowshoeing is it. Too few children get a chance to see their elders out there, enjoying the snow right alongside them. This is your chance to prove that we old folks know how to have a good time too. We live in Minnesota; we may as well enjoy what we've got—and we've got snow!

A word to the wise:

Snowshoe-making was a skill taught by American Indians, and it's a great way to make snowshoeing a little extra-special for your grandchild. Buy a kit and make your snowshoes together. You can also check the DNR website for state park activities. For instance, Jay Cooke and Fort Snelling offer snowshoe-making workshops, and many state parks host snowshoe hikes led by park naturalists.

Age of grandchild: 10 and up

Best season: Winter

Contact: Minnesota DNR (snowshoeing);
www.dnr.state.mn.us/young_naturalists/snowshoeing

Also check out:

Recommended snowshoe destinations: Chippewa National Forest, Cut Foot Sioux, Magnetic Rock Trail, North Country Trail, Northern Light Lake Trail, North Shore Parks, Suomi Hills and Superior National Forest

Hiker Central's snowshoe resources: www.hikercentral.com/snowshoe

Sunshine is delicious, rain is refreshing, wind braces us up, snow is exhilarating; there's really no such thing as bad weather, only different kinds of good weather. JOHN RUSKIN

Rock Collecting

Is there anything better for children than a treasure hunt? Rock collecting is just that. While it isn't about finding and selling valuable stones, it is a search for treasure of another sort—the kind that is unique, beautiful and priceless.

Minnesota's glacial landscape offers an ample supply of rocks of interesting sizes, textures and values. Some are even considered semiprecious stones. However, like I said before, the value is not in the selling but in the finding. Grandchildren love to find things. They are far more curious than we adults.

Rock collecting can be done just about anywhere. The Lake Superior Agate is a common prize for Minnesota rock hunters. It is formed in the bubbles (vesicles) of volcanic rocks, the kind that flowed out of the basin more than 1.1 billion years ago. Today, these agates can be found on Lake Superior beaches, in the gravel on northern roads and in a number of places all the way to towns such as Moose Lake and Finlayson, along Interstate 35.

The other rocks of the north are called Superior Till, and most are made up of volcanic lavas such as basalt and rhyolite. There are granites and feldspars,

hunks of banded iron formations, jasper, quartz and occasionally the soft but fascinating Thompsonite, which looks like a pink and white eye. Thompsonite is located in a few places near Grand Marais.

Let's not forget the southern parts of the state. In the southeast, limestones have vugs (holes) where calcite forms crystals. These crystals can be quite beautiful, and if the cavity weathers completely the rocks are called geodes. Meanwhile, southwestern Minnesota is famous for the red rock: Pipestone. Granite fills the central part of the state and can be quite attractive, as can the quartzite and the gneiss found in the southwest.

To a child, most of these details probably don't matter much. For them, the joy comes from finding an interesting rock that they can show off. From streets and alleys to parks and even your own back yard, rocks are everywhere. Spend some time with your grandchild, searching with him for just the right "treasure."

Bonding and bridging:

If you were offered $1,000 for all of your family photographs, would you take it? What if you were offered $10,000? I wouldn't—the pictures are priceless to me. Yet if a stranger found my photo album lying on the street, it would mean nothing to him. This is an excellent illustration of value versus worth. Our photographs have no monetary value, but they have special meaning to us and thus hold great worth.

The same can be said of your grandchild's rock collection. Most people will look at it and see only rocks. But your grandchild took special care to find, examine and keep each of his rocks, making them invaluable to him. This is an excellent chance to discuss the idea that money isn't everything. We can all find happiness in the simplest forms, and just because an item doesn't cost a lot doesn't mean it's worthless. After all, being rich isn't about having the most; it's about loving what we have.

A word to the wise:

When it comes to rock collecting, timing is everything. The best time to look for Minnesota agates is in spring. During winter, the rush of ice uncovers fresh agates and other handsome rocks, which are revealed in the spring thaw. In contrast, spring is a bad time for going to quarries and cliffs, where the freezing and thawing action might loosen rocks. For these locations, summer is a better option.

Age of grandchild: 5 to 12

Best season: Spring and summer

Also check out:

Hill Annex Mine State Park, Calumet; (218) 247-7215
www.dnr.state.mn.us/state_parks/hill_annex_mine

Lilydale Park Permit Office, Saint Paul; (651) 632-5111;
www.stpaul.gov/depts/parks/userguide/lilydale.html

Minnesota DNR (recreational geology); www.dnr.state.mn.us/geologyrec

Soudan Underground Mine State Park, Soudan; (218) 753-2245;
www.dnr.state.mn.us/state_parks/soudan_underground_mine

Picnicking

Few words brought as much joy to my childhood as the phrase, "Let's have a picnic." It meant a trip to a park, exploring the outdoors and—more likely than not—spending time with my grandparents. For you and your grandchild, a picnic is a simple pleasure that can provide both of you with as much happiness as it did (and still does) for me.

A picnic means packing up food and dishes in a basket, bringing charcoal (if an outdoor grill is available) and a tablecloth. You'll need a cooler for the cold foods and beverages. Perhaps you'll also want to have a hotdish, which you can keep warm by wrapping in a dish towel. For my grandmother, that trick always seemed to work. Somehow she managed to keep her food piping hot for more than fifty miles!

A picnic is an especially good idea if you live a couple of hours away from your grandchild. Find a good halfway point, and plan your picnic there. It's a great reason to get together, and everyone will have a good time. You sit and eat in fresh, open air. You're surrounded by green plants and singing birds. You can take your time eating, you can sit in a folding chair and watch the child play, and you can go for a short walk.

A picnic can be just about anything you want it to be, as long as you are enjoying the outdoors. The only rule is no fast food! A real picnic involves preparation and anticipation. It's a time to eat home-cooked food, roam, talk and perhaps even swim. Of course, you can always go back for seconds too.

Realistically, not everyone has time to make meatloaf for a delicious picnic sandwich. If you're short on time, a trip to your local deli or a specialty food shop is a great alternative solution. Take their finest foods—like chicken, mashed potatoes and corn—to the park and enjoy it with your loved ones.

Picnicking is a simple pleasure that gets overlooked in our world of fast food, but perhaps it's the antidote most needed. Spill something? So what? Leave your stress at home, relax, and eat with your fingers.

Bonding and bridging:

The best thing about a picnic is that it takes a very ordinary, everyday occurrence and turns it into something special. We all eat meals every day, at least three of them I hope. It's something that is routine. But when you take that everyday event and add a little twist to it—like eating outside—it becomes memorable. You can challenge your grandchild in this way. Ask her to think of something common or boring that she does on a regular basis, and see if she can come up with a way to make it special. This little game not only helps your grandchild flex her creative muscles, but it's also a great way to help her make the most out of life.

A word to the wise:

There's nothing like an open fire to captivate a grandchild, so use this as the focus for conversation and sharing. Make the fire with downed and dead wood only, and use wood that is breakable so you don't need an axe or saw. Start with tinder and the right natural fuels. Once you get it going, ignite your grandchild's imagination with s'mores: graham crackers, chocolate bars and marshmallows toasted to a creamy softness!

Age of grandchild: All

Best season: Spring, summer and fall (though winter can be fun too)

Also check out:

Minnesota's best state parks for picnics: Buffalo River, Camden, Glacial Lakes, Gooseberry, Itasca, Maplewood, Mille Lacs Kathio, Minneopa and William O'Brien. For more information, visit the website www.dnr.state.mn.us/state_parks

Berry Picking

Does picking berries take you back in time like it does for me? I can't smell blackberry pie or taste blackberry jam without thinking of my grandmother. Picking berries is one of those timeless rituals that transcends generations. Our grandparents did it with us, we can do it with our grandchildren, and they will likely do it with theirs.

When I was a child, my grandmother and I picked berries every summer— getting scratched, fighting off deer flies and coming back with two buckets from the berry patch. But it wasn't just the picking that made it memorable. It was also the way we ate the berries: pies cooling on a wire holder, coffee cake that no one has ever duplicated and so on. Just writing about it brings back memories of the rich, tasty berries filling my mouth with sweetness that's beyond words. This was the taste of sunshine and rain, of green plants and blue skies.

The tastes, smells, textures and colors, the outdoors and excellent company— nothing beats berry picking, and we are very lucky in Minnesota because our variety of berries is second to none.

Strawberries, raspberries and Grandma's favorite blackberries are all excellent choices. Raspberries aren't as rich as strawberries and aren't as virulent or as seed-laden as blackberries, but they are as refreshing as a berry can be. After all, who wouldn't enjoy a glass of raspberry liqueur, raspberry fruit wine or some delicious raspberry jam?

Let's not forget the fourth Minnesota favorite. You and your grandchild can find it in the sandy forests, growing around Jack pine and red pine trees. It's on a low, woody shrub that lacks thorns, that grows taller than strawberries and is filled with so many nutrients that some consider it the blue vitamin pill. Of course, I'm referring to the blueberry! Did you know that the Minnesota state muffin is the blueberry muffin?

Regardless of the flavor you choose, picking berries is a wonderful way to spend a morning or an afternoon. It gets you outside, allows you to spend time with your grandchild and ends with some delicious food to eat!

Bonding and bridging:

There are few activities that combine so many senses as picking berries. We smell, we touch, we see, and we taste. Take a moment with your grandchild to appreciate each of your senses. Make a game of it. Ask him to concentrate on one sense only, then ask him what he feels, tastes or smells.

This is a great exercise for helping your grandchild become more in tune with each of his senses. It raises his awareness of his surroundings, and it helps him learn to better appreciate the world he lives in.

A word to the wise:

Plan your summer to sample all four of Minnesota's berries. (They come in sequence: strawberry and blueberry, then raspberry and finally blackberry.) As part of your experiences, include food preparation and freezing the berries. Otherwise, our generation of grandparents may be the last to remember the canned goods in the pantry and the real jams and jellies.

Age of grandchild: 6 and up

Best season: Summer

Also check out:

The Minnesota Department of Agriculture publishes an annual guide to Minnesota-grown produce, including berry farms. Their *Minnesota Grown* directory is seasonally available in a number of places, from greenhouses and food co-ops to farmer's markets. You can call the Minnesota Department of Agriculture at (651) 201-6510 or visit them online at their website: www.mda.state.mn.us/mngrown

Our mothers and grandmothers...[move] to music not yet written. ALICE WALKER

Maple Syruping

What do we do in melt season, as winter is ending and spring is on its way? Follow your nose! That's right, the best scent in the forest takes place in late winter/early spring. It is the smell of maple steam rising from the evaporators and the concentration of natural sugars into one of our most traditional sweeteners: maple syrup.

It may be hard to remember—let alone explain—but white, processed sugar was not the original sweet of the Minnesota landscape. The Dakota and the Ojibwe Indians both made maple sugar, a process that is an extension of the syrup-making that pioneers engaged in. Vermont may claim to be the maple syrup capital of the country. But Minnesota has the Big Woods, the maple and basswood forests that once towered over the state's metropolitan, and the maple forests that follow the St. Croix River and its tributaries.

The process is simple, but very labor intensive:

1. Locate a maple tree that is more than ten inches in diameter.

2. Tap the tree (drill a hole) to divert the natural flow of sap.

3. Put in a spile (insert) for buckets, plastic bags or plastic tubes, depending upon how you're collecting the sap.

4. Wait twenty-four hours, then collect the sap.

5. When you have enough sap, boil it to concentrate the sugars.

6. When it reaches the right temperature or specific gravity, get it off the flame and filter it.

7. The maple syrup is finished.

That's it! The process sounds simple, but let's do the math. Syrup producers boil off thirty-nine parts out of every forty they collect. If they want to make ten gallons of syrup, it will take four hundred gallons of sap to do it. Aside from putting in the taps and taking them out, they still have to collect the sap each day. The weight of four hundred gallons of sap is a little more than 3,200 pounds!

Bonding and bridging:

When you look at something like the process of making maple syrup, at first it may seem quite complex. But it isn't. In fact, if you had the right tools and if you followed the procedure step by step, you'd find the entire experience to be fairly simple (except for all of the heavy lifting).

The same can be said for many challenges that arise in life. When your grandchild is faced with a difficult task or an overwhelming school assignment, remind her of maple syruping. If she equips herself with the right tools and breaks the task into smaller, simpler steps she can overcome any obstacle.

A word to the wise:

Try some sap, unprocessed, straight from the tree. Then try the taste of syrup. It's hard to believe that nothing was added. The only difference is that the water was removed. The best way to finish this experience is to eat some pancakes with maple syrup on them. Remember: It takes a lot less real syrup than artificial stuff to achieve the right taste.

Age of grandchild: 5 and up

Best season: February to April (depending upon the weather)

Contact: Minnesota Department of Agriculture; www.mda.state.mn.us

Also check out:

Audubon Center of the North Woods, Sandstone; (320) 245-2648; www.audubon-center.com

Brambleberry Farm, Pequot Lakes; (218) 568-8483

Carpenter St. Croix Valley Nature Center, Hastings; (651) 437-4359; www.carpenternaturecenter.org

Hamel Maple Syrup, Hamel; (763) 478-2353

Jake's Syrups, Vergas; (218) 863-2508

Wild Country Maple Syrup, Lutsen; (877) 663-8010; www.wildcountrymaple.com

Farmer's Market

In 1900 forty percent of Americans lived on farms, so almost everyone had an uncle, father or brother who was a farmer. By 1990 the number of farmers in America dropped to 1.9 percent. Most young people today don't have the experience of caring for animals, picking food for the evening's dinner or even running free in the pasture. Farms that remain have increased in size, and demand for more goods at cheaper prices requires mechanization.

How do we get children to understand what farming is and how important country land is to our survival? One of the best methods is with a visit to a community farmer's market. The colorful tables of produce, flowers, meats and baked goods are as close as many children will get to being at a farm.

Go early and wander leisurely. There is often music, sometimes samples and almost always a booth selling food and drinks. The smells, sounds, textures and colors are images that will stay with your grandchild—just as these images have stayed with me. Even the plants—touching and smelling them—can add to your grandchild's knowledge of the farmer's world.

There are so many lessons in this visit. Think about all of the contrasts between a farmer's market and a supermarket, such as the packaging (or lack thereof). Do we really even need packaging? Also consider what healthy food is and what the word "organic" means.

The beauty of the farmer's market is that you can ask these questions of the people selling their vegetables and fruits. They may not be able to answer all of them, but they can fill in a lot of the unknowns about the foods we eat.

Additionally, many of the urban markets now include vendors from different countries and cultures. You may not even recognize some of the produce they are selling. It is good for our grandchildren to see us engaging these people in conversation and asking them questions about their vegetables. It can be a great learning experience for both generations.

Farmer's markets can be found in most areas across the state. The cost of admission is only as much as you want to spend on delicious, fresh food, and the environment is "ripe" with potential for learning.

Bonding and bridging:

It's easy to take food for granted. Whenever we
want it, we know where to get it. A simple trip to
the grocery store takes care of our needs. Rarely
do we consider the question, "Where does this
food come from?"

A farmer's market is a chance to open your grandchild's eyes
to the hard work and dedication that go into everything we eat. He can
meet some of the people who work tirelessly, so we have food.

Tell him how important farmers are to our way of life. Share with him
how difficult growing crops truly is and how we would struggle if there
were no farmers to supply us with food. For older children, you may
also want to bring up third-world countries in which food supplies are
scarce. Either way, this is definitely a time when you want to help your
grandchild learn to appreciate his every meal.

A word to the wise:

Ask your grandchild to think about what he'd like to have for lunch, then
make your visit one of finding the best ingredients—it can become a treasure
hunt. Even the pickiest eater probably likes tomatoes, corn on the cob or
watermelon. To complete the morning's excursion, let him choose a bouquet
of freshly cut flowers to put on the table during your meal.

Age of grandchild: All

Best season: Late spring, summer and early fall

Contact: Agricultural Marketing Service (Minnesota's farmer's markets);
www.ams.usda.gov/farmersmarkets/states/minnesota.htm

Also check out:

The Minnesota Department of Agriculture publishes an annual guide to
Minnesota-grown produce, including farmer's markets. Their *Minnesota
Grown* directory is seasonally available in a number of places, including
greenhouses and food co-ops. You can also check it out online at
www.mda.state.mn.us/mngrown

Midwest Natural Foods Co-ops; www.mwnaturalfoods.coop

*Through my grandmother's eyes, I can see more clearly
the way things used to be, the way things ought to be, and
most important of all, the way things really are.* ED CUNNINGHAM

Classic and Antique Car Show

We are a car nation (and we're not talking about the flower). Mr. Ford did more than make it possible for every family to have a Model T. He set our nation on a path that would create a frenzy and love affair like nothing else in history. It might have been a rich man's toy to begin with and a working man's transportation through the next generations, but ultimately cars became an expression of who we are.

I'm not what you call a "car guy," but I still love to see the automobiles of my generation. My father was a mechanic. He loved the motor and the sound of his ratchet set clanking under the hood, but he couldn't pass his passion on to me. Instead, he had my daughter forsaking her dolls and playing with trucks and cars.

The automobiles of each generation reflect the society and the values of that time. Ford's Model T was a symbol of progress and innovation. In the 1950s, the Thunderbird represented status and pride. Today, we have trucks and Hummers demonstrating power, and even a nod to the classics with the ever-popular PT Cruiser.

Of course, a good car show features plenty of vintage automobiles. But it should also be about more than just the vehicles. You'll know you've found a good one if it feels like a festival. The event should include food, music and perhaps even awards. A parade is a must! There's nothing like finding a great spot near the curb of a city street and watching the amazing vehicles roll by. That's a trip down memory lane!

An antique car show is a collection of vehicles, but it is also filled with stories and memories of our youths. Lead your grandchild around the cars and share stories of the good ol' days with her, but don't be surprised if she finds a different car that sparks her imagination. She only has the shape and color to influence her, while you have memories.

Any time we can get our grandchildren excited about the past, we should seize the opportunity. An event that features plenty of fun activities—not to mention cool, old cars (which most kids love)—is just the ticket.

Bonding and bridging:

Cars always have been and always will be special.
Driving your first car is a right of passage—a
sign that a child is becoming an adult. Yet our
infatuation with cars is about something even
greater. Cars become pieces of our own identities.
Especially for teenagers, cars represent independence
and individuality. Not all of us got to choose the make, model and color
of our first cars, but it didn't matter. We made those cars a reflection of
who we were.

For your grandchild, a car symbolizes a longing to be an adult and a
desire to create her own identity. You can't move time forward, but you
can start talking with her about her "dream" car. Ask her what kind of
car she would want and what color. You may even decide to bring her to
a car lot in order to look at the variety. Allowing your grandchild to
make choices such as these gives her an outlet for her desire to become
her own individual.

A word to the wise:

The Back to the Fifties Show at the State Fair is the classiest of the classics:
big fins, big motors and lots of horses under the hood. Enjoy one of the
biggest car shows in the region. Best of all, when you've finished exploring all
of the vintage cars, you can partake in the food, fun and games that the State
Fair has to offer!

Age of grandchild: All

Best season: Spring, summer and fall

Also check out:

Midwest Car Shows; www.midwestcarshows.com

Cemetery Visit

Not every activity that you choose to share with your grandchild will be an exciting trip to a fun and far off place. Sometimes you'll find a worthwhile destination close to home. A trip to a cemetery may not be at the top of your list, but there are some lessons that you can share better than anyone else, and a cemetery visit is one chance to do it.

For children, a grandparent's death may be the first great loss in their lives. It is not necessary to have a "when I die" talk with your grandchild, but you should let the fact of death be part of your life. That will make it easier for your grandchild when the day comes.

Cemeteries offer many lessons, and it will be a good experience for both of you, if you're the one who helps him learn them. Choose an old cemetery, one that reflects on history and events. Look at the monuments, but visit the gravestones.

Find the headstones and check their dates. If you are in an old cemetery you might find stones that commemorate children who died of diphtheria, small-pox or one of any number of diseases. These are lessons in good health, good hygiene and good medicine. It may comfort your grandchild to know that, when he takes his preventative medicines and shots, it is because we do not want to face these tragic epidemics ever again.

What are the names in the cemetery? Are they names you recognize? Can you find stories of military deaths, fires, plagues or other events that affected the community? The grounds are sure to offer plenty of history lessons, with comparisons of why we live longer today than we would have fifty, seventy-five or one hundred years ago.

Most children view cemeteries as dark, scary places. By visiting one together, you are helping your grandchild discover that it's okay to celebrate someone's life, even after death. Plus, you're showing him that a visit to a cemetery can be a reflective activity and one that's quite enjoyable.

Bonding and bridging:

The death of a loved one is a traumatic experience for anyone; it's even harder for a child. A visit to a cemetery is a chance to help your grandchild understand that death is a natural end to life. Talk openly about it. If you are a spiritual person, discuss your beliefs in the afterlife. Make it easy for him to ask questions. Let him know that the topic of death is not taboo. If you approach the subject with the right mix of honesty and tact, you will make it easier for your grandchild to overcome his grief when the day comes that he loses someone special, perhaps even you.

A word to the wise:

Bring a large piece of paper and chalk (or charcoal). Place the paper over an old gravestone, and rub the chalk over the paper against it. The words and images should transfer without doing any damage. This is a unique art project that your grandchild can take home.

Age of grandchild: 10 and up

Best season: Fall

Also check out:

Hinckley Cemetery (honoring the 1894 fire victims), Hinckley

Minneapolis Pioneers and Soldiers Memorial Cemetery, Minneapolis; www.friendsofthecemetery.org

Minnesota Association of Cemeteries, Minneapolis; (612) 822-2171; www.mncemeteries.org

Sunrise Cemetery (with a large number of Civil War fatalities); Sunrise

Even now, I am not old. I never think of it, and yet I am a grandmother to eleven grandchildren. GRANDMA MOSES

Bird Watching

In America, bird watching is a growing activity. There is renewed interest in birds and in discovering how to find and record them. This interest seems to grow stronger as we grow older. On the other end of the spectrum, children have an intense interest in birds too. They will spend hours watching birds at the feeder, trying to identify and draw them.

Most young grandchildren are instinctively curious naturalists. Birds happen to be colorful and easier to see than other types of animals. So sitting in front of a group of feeders can be among the most enjoyable and action-filled events that you share.

To optimize your experience together, plan ahead. Schedule a time of day in which you are most likely to see the types of birds you want to see. Have a *Birds of Minnesota* field guide on hand, as well as pencils and paper for taking notes and drawing. If your grandchild is interested in photography, you may want to have a camera available too. Taking notes, looking up and identifying birds create valuable skills and a feeling of ownership over that moment and observation.

To attract a variety of birds, the perfect combination of feeders includes a good hummingbird feeder, a thistle feeder, a suet feeder and a platform feeder for sunflowers and nuts. The variety of feeders brings colorful birds in close and eliminates the need to use binoculars.

Filling the feeders is another ritual that your grandchild will likely enjoy sharing with you. Put out a few kinds of seeds in special locations each morning. It will connect you and your grandchild with your feathered regulars. In the winter, chickadees can be conditioned to feed from your grandchild's hand. In the summer, a mealworm feeder and a water bath improve observation chances and increase your number of species.

Childhood discoveries can lead to careers—or at least to hobbies. Many times these discoveries plant seeds that mature as we grow, setting us on a path that ultimately affects our entire futures. As we get older, we have more time to reflect on what is real and what is valuable.

Bonding and bridging:

Seeing old birds through new eyes is a wonderful experience. It makes the robin more vibrant, the goldfinch glow and the nuthatch hilarious.

Teaching your grandchild how to watch birds and helping her make her own discoveries are rewarding for you and for her. The field guide becomes a tool, as she learns that books contain knowledge. She begins to make lists of birds that she has seen, as well as notes about her observations. Before either of you truly realize what is happening, your granddaughter is on a path of discovery about scientific thoughts and methods.

A word to the wise:

Cornell Lab of Ornithology has a number of citizen science programs including the Great Backyard Bird Count. By participating in this activity, you and your grandchild are participating in a real science experiment. You will connect your feeders to other feeders throughout North America, giving a greater meaning to your shared experiences. Check out the website below to join.

Age of grandchild: All

Best season: All

Contact: The Great Backyard Bird Count;
citizenscience@audubon.org • www.birdsource.org/gbbc

Also check out:

Eastman Nature Center, Maple Grove; (763) 694-7700; www.threeriversparkdistrict.org/outdoor_ed/center_eastman.cfm

Lowry Nature Center, Victoria; (763) 694-7650; www.threeriversparkdistrict.org/outdoor_ed/center_lowry.cfm

Minnesota DNR (bird feeding); www.dnr.state.mn.us/birdfeeding

Minnesota River Valley National Wildlife Refuge, Bloomington; (952) 854-5900; www.nps.gov/miss/maps/model/mnrefuge.html

One way to open your eyes is to ask yourself,
"What if I had never seen this before? What if
I knew I would never see it again?" RACHEL CARSON

Fishing

One thing is certain: Minnesota is fishing country! This great state of ours is peppered with lakes and rivers at every turn. The desire to grab a rod, hop into a boat and hit the water is a longing that many people feel every day. If there's a more "Minnesota" activity to share with your grandchild than the thrill of fishing, I can't imagine what it might be.

I have to confess: I'm not much of a fisherman. I know it sounds crazy to live in Minnesota and not be, but that's just the way I am. However, I understand the appeal. As a lover of the outdoors, I can see why someone might choose to spend his free time in a boat or along a shore, at one with nature, relaxing and absorbing the sights and sounds. Fishing is something that Minnesotans do, and it's a must for you to introduce your grandchild to it.

There are plenty of options for fishing. If you have a boat, that's the best way to go. Bring your grandchild into the middle of a lake, drop anchor, bait his hook and let the fun begin. Teach him a few tricks—such as casting and reeling. Show him how to tell if a fish is on the line. Most importantly, keep your fishing trip short and fun. For many young children, boat fishing is more about the ride than it is about catching any fish.

You can also fish from a beach or dock. The greatest benefits of shore fishing are that bored children can run and play, and bathrooms are more accessible. The trick to shore fishing is to keep moving. Wander along the shoreline, casting to various spots until you find a good place where the fish are biting. Deep water and shady locations are usually the best fishing areas.

During the winter months, ice fishing is a wonderful Minnesota tradition. Once again, for young children, they'll likely have more fun running around and playing on the ice than they will waiting for a fish to bite. You can always hold your grandchild's rod for him and give a holler when he gets a tug on his line. As soon as he reels in that first catch, he'll be hooked for life!

A great Minnesota custom, a chance to be outside and the opportunity to spend time with your grandchild—fishing is a recreation that offers it all!

Bonding and bridging:

All great fishermen have one trait in common: patience. Fishing isn't a thrill-a-minute, instant-gratification kind of activity. It's about staying calm, relaxing and anticipating the moment when you feel a tug on the line.

A fishing trip is a chance to introduce your grandchild to the concept of patience. He may get bored, but encourage him to wait just a little while longer. When he finally hauls in a fish, his excitement level will be unmatched—demonstrating to him that some things are worth the wait.

A word to the wise:

If you know as much (or as little) about fishing as I do, you and your grandchild may benefit from the services of a fishing guide. A guide will lead you to the best fishing spots in your area, as well as show you the ins and outs of fishing. Another option is a charter fishing tour—perfect for large groups. All you need is a fishing license, and they'll take care of the rest.

Age of grandchild: 5 and up

Best season: Spring (more fish are caught per hour than during any other season)

Also check out:

Fishing Minnesota (fishing guides);
www.fishingminnesota.com/fishing-guides.html

Minnesota DNR (fishing); www.dnr.state.mn.us/fishing

One hundred years from now, it will not matter what my bank account was, how big my house was, or what kind of car I drove. But the world may be a little better because I was important in the life of a child. FOREST WITCRAFT

Kite Flying

Not every activity needs a great amount of planning, expensive tickets and cheering crowds. Sometimes you just need open space and wind. After all, an afternoon of flying a kite is an afternoon well spent.

Flight is in our dreams, in our cultural history and in our world's vision of the future. If you are looking for a simple activity that connects your grandchild to wind, energy and flight, it is hard to beat flying a kite.

Out in that field or park, it is just your grandchild, you and that simple object on a string. Your grandchild can run, laugh and feel that slight tug and lift. When the kite finally gets airborne, it's all sun, breeze and smiles. Simple yet profound, this childhood toy is a connection to history, science and joy.

Marco Polo brought kites from China to the Western world, and the West found practical ways to use them. Alexander Wilson flew his thermometers on his kites, Ralph Archbold flew anemometers, and Benjamin Franklin survived a really dumb experiment: flying a kite in a lightning storm. Ships released kites if they were in danger, hoping that rescue would result. Kites were also flown from life rafts to help rescuers spot drifting boats.

I still have childhood memories of a clear sunny day with gusty winds, standing atop a hill in Minneapolis. My parents and grandparents had purchased a box kite, and we had assembled it together. I anticipated the excitement. I ran and ran and ran. At last the kite took flight, and we had great fun, playing out the string, watching it rise, feeling the surge.

When we see the colorful kites of today—flying along Lake Superior, in the windy southwest or in a green city park—it reminds us that some pleasures have not disappeared. Flying a kite is, in fact, still a viable happiness to be shared. It not only bridges sky and earth but generations of dreamers.

Bonding and bridging:

Can you think of an activity more pleasurable and simple than running across a grass field, string in hand, kite taking flight? It is the essence of a shared experience with your grandchild. It is not money, glitz or glamour that connects us but rather the quiet sharing of discovery.

What is flight? What is wind? What does the kite teach us about flight? Kite flying is a perfect opportunity to talk with your grandchild about Wilbur and Orville Wright, da Vinci and all of the dreamers of flight who steered us toward modern planes and rockets. The kite is a thread to the sky. It was Ben Franklin's means to learn about lightning; maybe it is your grandchild's means to explore her dreams about the universe.

A word to the wise:

If you are looking for a kite experience that is almost magical, help your grandchild build her own with string, ribbon, newspaper and wood. Can she imagine those ingredients taking her into the atmosphere? How should she shape the kite? Why a tail? This is a great way to start; later you can graduate to more elaborate designs. However, your grandchild's feeling of putting a piece of paper into her own little orbit is very exciting, and to build it with her grandparent is truly precious.

Age of grandchild: 5 and up

Best season: Spring, summer and fall

Also check out:

American Kitefliers Association; (800) 252-2550; www.aka.kite.org

Faribault Airfest, Faribault; (800) 658-2354
(Faribault Area Chamber of Commerce); www.faribaultairfest.com

How to Go and Fly a Kite; www.skratch-pad.com/kites

Minnesota Kite Flying Club; www.mnkites.org

Life is no brief candle to me. It is a sort of splendid torch which I've got hold of for the moment and I want to make it burn as brightly as possible before handing it on to the future generations. GEORGE BERNARD SHAW

Library

From Sumerians to ancient Egyptians, the library has existed in many forms for thousands of years. It is a location that collects knowledge in writing. Few places hold so much potential for so many. Inside you can discover stories of love and adventure or detailed information about porpoises, the Eiffel Tower and countless other topics. All of this, and you can find a library in almost every Minnesota town.

A trip to the library is a magical experience for your grandchild. At the bookstore, he's not allowed to touch. At home, he's already seen and read those books. But as soon as he walks through the library doors, he has the world at his fingertips.

Give your grandchild time to explore and to find a book (or two) that excites him. Guide him if he needs help. You can search for books together based on a series that he enjoys, an author he likes or a subject matter that is of particular interest. Let him absorb the library's atmosphere. This is a places where book lovers congregate, where a passion for reading can be observed and mimicked.

Do your part, and set an example too. Check out a few books before you leave. Don't spend too much time browsing for yourself. (It's best if you already know what you're looking for.) But if you leave with a handful of books, your grandchild will notice. He may even ask what you're reading, and from there the conversation can soar.

Libraries offer several other opportunities too. From time to time, children's authors make appearances. It's always a thrill for children to meet the writers who create the characters and worlds they read about. Libraries occasionally host used book sales—a chance to help your local library raise funds, and most of the books cost no more than a dollar!

A library visit holds unlimited potential—so much so, that it may be worth repeating with your grandchild every week.

Bonding and bridging:

There is little you can do for your grandchild that is more important than instilling in him a love of reading. Books are our sources for a history of knowledge, and a child who loves to read is a child who loves to learn.

For your grandchild, a trip to the library means he gets to choose a book that will make him laugh, cry or go on a wild adventure. Help him discover stories that will get him hooked on reading. Learn what his interests are, and lead him to books that pertain to the topic. The sooner you begin taking him to the library, the better. Even before he can read on his own, allow him to choose books that the two of you can enjoy together.

A word to the wise:

A visit to the library can enhance just about any experience in this book. Of course, you can check out *On the Banks of Plum Creek* before visiting Walnut Grove. With older grandchildren, you may want to read *Main Street* before attending Sinclair Lewis Days. And let's not forget *The Wizard of Oz* to supplement the Judy Garland Museum. But there are many other possibilities too. Get a book on eagles before traveling to the National Eagle Center. Read about American Indians before visiting the Mille Lacs Indian Museum or the Pipestone National Monument. Whatever the topic may be, you have a world of books to choose from.

Age of grandchild: All

Best season: All

Also check out:

Your local bookstores

Tea Party

Among the most powerful childhood memories I have of my mother is an event that she used to call, "Having a tea party with Mrs. McGillicuddy." I have no idea who Mrs. McGillicuddy was or how my mother came up with that name, but it succeeded in setting the tone for fun. I can't remember much else except my absolute, sheer delight and my amazement that Mom could act so silly and playful.

Unfortunately, in our culture, tea parties have a gender bias. (In contrast, men and women alike enjoy tea breaks and even something called high tea in the British Isles.) It may be difficult for you to sell a grandson on the idea of a tea party, but that's not to say you shouldn't try. Almost all kids love dressing up and play-acting, taking on the role of someone else, especially if that someone else is an adult character.

There are several options for tea parties. First, the grandchild may host a party for a collection of her favorite stuffed animals or dolls; second, she may host a party for a small group of friends; or third, adults such as parents and/or grandparents are the participants. You can help facilitate the first two—but to have the most fun, the third option is the best choice.

A good tea party involves dressing up in some old formalwear, sitting around a little table and drinking make-believe tea. Set the table with your good dishes or with child-sized plates and cups. Add a flower centerpiece, and maybe even make invitations if others will be attending. You may also want to choose new names for the party, something old-fashioned and formal. Adopt an accent. Ham it up. Find some funny, fancy clothes or hats to wear, and get ready for the fun to begin.

For more realism, make little sandwiches and desserts; your grandchild can help. Mix a variety of teas (those with a sweeter flavor are probably best), but have other beverages such as lemonade or juice handy.

Your grandchild will be amazed that you can act like someone else, and she will be tickled by your willingness to play this "game" with her. Giggles and laughter will erupt frequently—guaranteed.

Bonding and bridging:

Despite all of the play involved with a tea party, there are still lessons to be shared. In our society, civility and manners are being crushed under the weight of rude and disrespectful behavior. Use this time to demonstrate table etiquette, with the use of silverware and polite conversation. Teach your grandchild about old-fashioned manners in a playful way, and you'll be surprised how well it carries over to meal time. Plus, you'll both have a lot of fun, and your grandchild may even ask for a repeat performance.

A word to the wise:

Read the part of *Alice in Wonderland* where the Mad Hatter hosts a tea party. This may inspire future party ideas, as well as introducing the child to some classic literature. For another idea, you can find a number of restaurants and tea houses in the state that offer high tea. If the child demonstrates an ability to enjoy this kind of semiformal setting, you can include outings to these places as special events.

Age of grandchild: 5 and up

Best season: All

Also check out:

Afternoon Tea Party; www.afternoonteaparty.com

High Tea at many bed & breakfasts are open to the public and do not require overnight stays

High Tea at Murray's, Minneapolis; (612) 339-0909

North Shore Scenic Railroad Tea Train, Duluth (800) 423-1273; www.northshorescenicrailroad.org

Tea Time Traditions; www.seedsofknowledge.com/whimsy.html

Grandparents Day

I don't have to tell you that grandparents are special. We play an important part in the healthy development of our grandchildren, and we deserve a special day. Grandparents Day may not get the national recognition that Mother's Day and Father's Day receive, but it is a day that should be celebrated. It is a day that should be spent with your grandchild.

In 1973 Grandparents Day was first established in West Virginia, thanks to the efforts of Marian McQuade, a mother of fifteen who was as dedicated to the care of senior citizens as she was to children. She formed the Forget-Me-Not Ambassadors, ensuring that senior homes were visited regularly. President Jimmy Carter recognized this effort in 1978 and ushered in a national day of commemoration.

Grandparents Day takes place every September, on the first Sunday after Labor Day. It is a day that's all too easy to overlook since it follows the last big holiday of summer, at the beginning of the school year. It's up to you to ensure that the day is not forgotten. Plan a fun activity that you and your grandchild can share. Create traditions. If possible, have the child over to your place for a once-a-year special event.

The day is not about going somewhere for outside entertainment. Have a cake and celebrate, but concentrate on the things that made your childhood special. Play some old board games. Gather everyone around and tell stories from your childhood—but not for too long. Leave them wanting more. If you have any old clothing, a little dress-up can go a long way. You can even pop some popcorn and gather around the old radio.

Whatever you decide to do, make it a day where your grandchild can honor you and appreciate how important you are in his life. His parents can help make this happen, but it can also be a success if you do the planning. Grandparents Day is still a relatively unknown holiday; it's up to us to raise awareness of this worthy occasion.

Bonding and bridging:

In today's world, it can be hard for people to show their true feelings. Saying, "I love you," almost seems taboo. Why that is I do not know, but Grandparents Day is a good time to remember that it's okay to let your family members know that they are loved.

Practice saying, "I love you," not just on Grandparents Day but every day. Model the lifestyle of a person who tells the world how you feel. Your grandchild will notice, and when he reaches the age where telling his family he loves them and giving his grandparents a hug becomes "uncool," maybe he'll do it anyway.

A word to the wise:

Choose a special activity—such as baking cookies or flying a kite—that you can share with your grandchild every year at this time. Make sure it's something that you enjoy as much as your grandchild does. After all, this day is for you. Whatever you choose, it will become something that both of you look forward to every year, and it will help ensure that Grandparents Day is an annual, family tradition.

Age of grandchild: All

Best season: The first Sunday after Labor Day

Contact: Your place or your grandchild's home

Also check out:

Father's Day, the third Sunday in June

Mother's Day, the second Sunday in May

Grandchildren are the dots that connect the lines from generation to generation. LOIS WYSE

Index

About the Authors

Mike Link:

Mike Link is the author of seventeen books and numerous magazine articles. He and and his wife Kate live in the woods near Willow River, Minnesota, with two labrador retrievers and a feeder full of birds.

For more than thirty-five years, Mike has directed the Audubon Center near Sandstone, Minnesota, and he occasionally guides groups through the western national parks. He takes pride in teaching and enjoys sharing his knowledge about environmental subjects with the students at Hamline University, Northland College and others.

Traveling is a passion that Mike shares with Kate, one that has taken them to all fifty states and twenty countries. It is the author's belief that if you breathe air, drink water and enjoy life, you owe a debt to the future and must preserve and protect the world's environments.

Mike's son Matthew was a student at the University of Minnesota Duluth when he died in a kayak accident in New Zealand, and his son Jon is a kayak wilderness ranger near Juneau, Alaska. His daughters Julie and Alyssa have provided him with grandsons—Matthew, Aren and Ryan—who have given him the gift to see the world again through new eyes.

Kate Crowley:

For twenty-one years, Kate Crowley has lived her dream. Since marrying Mike and moving to the country, she has been surrounded by forests, prairies,

birds, dogs, cats and horses. Her dream was made complete when she became a grandmother.

Kate has been a naturalist, an educator and a writer for twenty-nine years, first at the Minnesota Zoo and now at the Audubon Center of the North Woods. She has co-authored nine books with Mike. She has written for magazines and currently writes a monthly nature column for three newspapers.

Kate enjoys hiking, biking, skiing, scrapbooking, reading and spending as much time as possible with her grandchildren. She considers protecting and preserving the natural world for her grandchildren and for future generations to be her highest priority.

Visit Mike and Kate's website at www.GrandparentsAmericanStyle.com

Notes

Date:

Comments: